ORDER AND AGENCY
IN MODERNITY

ORDER AND AGENCY IN MODERNITY

TALCOTT PARSONS, ERVING GOFFMAN, AND HAROLD GARFINKEL

Kwang-Ki Kim

State University of New York Press

Published by
State University of New York Press, Albany

For information, address State University of New York Press,
90 State Street, Suite 700, Albany, NY 12207

Production by Diane Ganeles
Marketing by Jennifer Giovani

Library of Congress Cataloging-in-Publication Data

Kim, Kwang-ki, 1963–
    Order and agency in modernity : Talcott Parsons, Erving Goffman, and Harold
Garfinkel / Kwang-ki Kim.
       p. cm.
    Includes bibliographical references and indexes.
    ISBN 0-7914-5539-4 (alk. paper)—ISBN 0-7914-5540-8 (pbk. : alk. paper)
       1. Parsons, Talcott, 1902– 2. Goffman, Erving. 3. Garfinkel, Harold. 4.
Sociology—History—20th century. 5. Civilization, Modern—Philosophy. I. Title.

HM447.K56 2003
301'.09'04—dc21   2002070467

10 9 8 7 6 5 4 3 2 1

To my parents,
Seiyoung and Kyunghee Kim
Who made it all possible!

Wo aber Gefahr ist, wächst
Das Rettende auch.

But where danger is, grows
The saving power also.

—Friedrich Hölderlin, *Patmos*

CONTENTS

PREFACE

The social conditions of Modernity are assuming more and ⁊ more extreme forms, with no indication of moderating. Modernity in its many historical and cultural transformations has touched virtually every culture and every person around the globe. Social science is following these developments, as it has from its very beginnings. The social conditions of Modernity are therefore the subject of continuing study and debate. I place myself in this academic context, but also in this socio-historical context, as both a citizen and a sociologist. I therefore find the problem of modernity to be not only an important subject of inquiry, but also an extremely interesting and engaging one, personally as well as professionally.

At the same time, much of my experience in sociological theory has revolved around another central set of problems, relating to ⌊human agency and social order.⌋ Both sets of problems have consumed my attention. After a number of years of studying these questions largely independently of one another, I developed a strong suspicion that the two issues must be addressed together, as intricately related phenomena. That is, I began to suspect that ⸸ human agency, social order, and their relation(s) assume special forms in the Modern period, that they become personally and theoretically problematic in decisively modern ways, and that they are available only in their modern forms, to modern minds.

These biographical details provide the personal basis for the present work. It is a work that synthesizes two sets of interests as a means of satisfying each more fully. This synthesis takes the form of a study in the relationship between modernity and modern sociological theory, the latter understood as a body of thought in which the problems of human agency and social order are central concerns. It is neither about modernity nor the relations between agency and order, but about how the two topics are related and how their studies can inform one another.

꙳ The present work began as my doctoral dissertation in sociology at Boston University, and now includes additional material, expanding upon the original focus of my dissertation. It is a pleasure to acknowledge those who have supported my work over the years in which this project developed, as I researched and wrote my dissertation and subsequently, as I have revisited the dissertation and expanded its scope. I owe my greatest intellectual debt to Peter Berger, my teacher and dissertation supervisor. He has been the personification of academic generosity, and he has taught me much, both directly and indirectly. Without his unlimited support and guidance this work would hardly have been possible, and I remain profoundly grateful to him. I also want to express my deepest gratitude to George Psathas, who opened the doors to new fields of experience, from academic specializations to baseball at Fenway Park. His scholarship and his friendship have always been inspiring and helpful. I would also like to acknowledge other faculty in the Department of Sociology at Boston University for their encouragement. Particularly, I am grateful to Jeff Coulter for sharing his rigorous intellect and his friendship; he propelled me to take a close look at a world previously seen but unnoticed. I also want to thank Stephen Kalberg, Brigitte Berger, and Annemette Sørensen for being encouraging and dedicated mentors. I owe a word of thanks to Tim Berard, my friend and Theory Twin, who has sustained a conversation about our shared concerns and interests since we met, and who sacrificed his own time to persistently discuss, carefully read, and critically comment on my manuscript; my writing has benefited at many points from his scholarly readings. Needless to say, none of these people are responsible for any errors. Those that remain in the text are my own.

Several other people have also provided encouragement and support at various times during my graduate studies and beyond. I remain deeply grateful to Erazim Kohák, Adam B. Seligman, Murray Melbin, Michael Lynch, Jonghoe Yang, Hyun-ho Seok, Chang-soo Chung, Yunjong Shim, Hungmo Yang, Hagen Koo, Herbert Barringer, Peter Manicas, Alvin So, Karen Joe, Douglas Bwy, and no doubt others who I am unintentionally failing to mention. I would also like to express my thanks to the three anonymous readers for State University of New York Press for their interest in my work and the suggestions that led me to elaborate upon my dissertation.

I must also express my gratitude to my family, including my parents Seiyoung and Kyunghee Kim, my lovely wife Namju, my daughter Ah-hyun Ruth, my brother Kwanghui, my sister Heiyun and her husband Insu Han, and my wife's family, especially my wife's parents Jeongdae and Sangja Joo, and her sister Namyeon, for their endless support, love, prayers, and smiles. I have saved until last a word of acknowledgment for the musicians who enliven the Park Street subway station in Boston; they repeatedly provided an oasis for me during a period in my life when I was often exhausted and alone with my work.

Kwang-ki Kim

INTRODUCTION

I begin with the question, 'what is "modern" about "modern sociological theory"?' Why should we put the adjective 'modern' in front of some 'sociological theory'? Is it only because it has appeared in the modern period? This is a reason, but not the best reason, I think. A more fundamental reason, in my judgment, is that there is a strong substantive relationship between 'modernity' and 'modern sociological theory.' Sociology is deeply articulated with, or implicated in, 'modernity.'[1]

Different aspects of this relationship have been noted many times before. Berger and Kellner, for example, observe that sociology has been "transfixed from the very beginning by modernity as a topic of inquiry," and they describe sociology as a "peculiarly modern discipline in its approach and methods" (1981, 15). Bellah and his colleagues note the wide acceptance of the view that modernity and sociology (or social science) were "born together" and that "their fates are deeply intertwined" (1983,1). The concern with modernity is actually evident in a wide range of sociological theory. Indeed, many of the most respected sociological theorists have wrestled with the question of modernity, from classical theorists (e.g., Pareto, Marx, Weber, Simmel, and Durkheim) to post-World War II and contemporary theorists (e.g. Parsons, members of the Frankfurt School, Berger, Habermas, and Giddens).

This literature serves as evidence for my contention that modern sociological theory is modern in more than just a superficial sense, but my interest is not in outlining the history of the study of modernity in sociological theory, nor even in discussing the efforts of specific figures to theorize modernity. I have a more specific interest in studying modernity in its relation to our theoretical understanding of agency and order, and the above-mentioned inquiries into modernity would touch on these questions only accidentally. So instead of focusing on prominent contemporary critics of modernity, such as Habermas or Lyotard, I would like to focus on *modern features* of the works of three theorists who are not in themselves famous for theorizing or critiquing modernity: Talcott Parsons, Erving Goffman, and Harold Garfinkel.

Parsons, Goffman, and Garfinkel are not famous for addressing modernity, but rather for [having defined many of the parameters for the debate about human agency and social order.] These three theorists, however, reveal a profound interest in social conditions that must be seen as peculiarly or especially *modern*. One only needs to look beyond the most explicit studies of modernity in order to find modernity in a range of theories where it is addressed less explicitly, but sometimes to greater effect. My basic approach, then, will be to develop the argument that Parsons, Goffman, and Garfinkel deserve to be recognized as leading theorists in the tradition of modern sociological theory, that is, in the theoretical understanding of modern society.

This approach will likely be met with some skepticism, due to the fact that these three figures, and especially Goffman and Garfinkel, did not study modernity per se. One criticism that deserves special mention is the criticism leveled against all three theorists at different times, that their contributions suffer from a lack of historical perspective (see, e.g., Gouldner 1970). I do not want to argue this point, but rather to illustrate how each of the three theoretical treatments of order and agency is importantly informed by and concerned with modern social conditions, regardless of their comparative-historical credentials. Ethnomethodologists might be especially skeptical due to their general aversion to theorizing, especially macro-theorizing.[2] But my primary interest is in developing a richer understanding of leading contributions to the study of social order and human agency, and in drawing out neglected points of comparison between these contributions. I therefore hope my readings of these three theorists' works will be recognized as respectful readings, even though I don't read these contributions at face value or adhere to their methodological tenets in my analysis.

Parsons must be distinguished from Goffman and Garfinkel in some of these respects. Despite the frequent criticism that his theoretical system was 'static', he did deal with historical questions at times, and he came much closer than Goffman and Garfinkel to offering explicit analyses of modern society, as such. But with Parsons as well as with Goffman and Garfinkel, my interest will be to unearth the implicit understanding of modernity that inform the attempts to theorize human agency and social order.

Regardless of the many important differences between the three theorists, each is concerned with the reality of human collective life. Because modernity is deeply sedimented in this reality, insightful theories of social life written during the modern period cannot help but reflect modern social conditions. So all three theorists end up dealing with modernity, and at a similarly implicit level of analysis, despite the differences between them in the degree to which they discuss modernity and in their theoretical treatments of agency and order.

One could call my project a "sociology of knowledge" approach to sociological theory, in which I read contributions to sociological theory in light of their modern context. This would be appropriate, but my project is also motivated by a desire to illustrate that the study of modernity should not be relegated to the status of an esoteric specialization, one aligned with, for example, the sociology of developing countries or the sociology of culture. In answering the question, "what makes modern sociological theory modern?", I will be trying to shed light on much more than an esoteric substantive question; I will be offering an analysis which simultaneously addresses the social conditions of sociological thought, the works of three leading sociological theorists, and the substantive topics of human agency and social order, with each dimension of the analysis informing the others.

The outline of the project will be as follows. I will begin by referring to some of the most general characteristics of modernity, as they are deliberately and acutely identified and explored by sociologists such as Simmel, Gehlen, Schelsky, Zijderveld, Natanson, Seligman, Luckman, and Berger. My approach to the problem of modernity is essentially a macro approach, but in a cultural rather than a structural sense. A concern with the experience of modernity is a macro concern, but one that is not often addressed in comparative-historical, political and economic sociology. I will have occasion to discuss more conventional macro or structural approaches to modernity, including those of Weber, Marx, Durkheim, and Fromm, but I will be interested in relating their concerns, concerns such as rationalization, alienation, anomie, and individualism, to my own phenomenological concerns with modernity as a cultural phenomenon. Indeed, rationalization, alienation, anomie, and individualism are all cultural aspects of modernity that classical theorists chose to explain in largely structural terms.

After outlining this general understanding of modernity, I will then proceed to suggest that characteristics of modernity assume an important if implicit role in the works of Parsons, Goffman, and Garfinkel. These issues will occupy my attention in chapters 2, 3, and 4, respectively. In each of these chapters, I will explicate the understanding of modernity implicit in each body of theory, with special reference to the questions of human agency and social order. Following this, I will offer a brief comparison of these bodies of theory as variants on modern sociological theory. In these respects I hope to suggest new possibilities for nuanced, meaningful comparisons between theoretical traditions that are too often divided by means of heavy-handed and stereotypical contrasts. Throughout I will forward the argument that our understanding of modern sociological theory, and its treatments of agency and social order especially, can be improved by reading canonical texts as expressions or illustrations of modern social conditions and the tensions between them.

1

ON MODERNITY

In this chapter, I will attempt to delineate some characteristics of modernity. Needless to say, there are a great number of studies outlining the characteristics of modernity. But it cannot be my task here to review and synthesize this enormous amount of material into a consistent theory. Instead, I will emphasize just two major characteristics of modernity here in order to relate them to Talcott Parsons's, Erving Goffman's, and Harold Garfinkel's theories of social order and agency: pluralism and abstraction. It should be noted, however, that these two major characteristics overlap, and are even inseparable. I shall also mention some additional characteristics of modernity: the mutual autonomization of the individual and the institutional order from each other, subjectivization, the weakening of roles and the growth of individualism, and the regression into, and emphasis upon, the 'hic et nunc' ('here and now'). Some of these additional characteristics can be seen as consequences of pluralism and abstraction.

MODERNITY IN CLASSICAL THEORY

Before looking at these characteristics of modernity, however, I will briefly address the treatment of modernity in classical sociological

1

theory. Specifically, I will review some relevant aspects of Marx's, Weber's, and Durkheim's theories of modern society, since these are widely appreciated as the landmark analyses of modernity in classical sociological theory. Simmel is another important figure in the classical tradition, but his discussion of modernity is excluded from this section since his analysis will be treated later, in my phenomenological approach to modernity.

Karl Marx's discussion of *alienation* (*Entfremdung*), is the *locus classicus* in modern sociological thinking of the concern with what I will call 'distancing,' a feature of modernity which will be emphasized in the analysis to follow. The concept of 'alienation' has at times enjoyed significant currency in political and professional discourse, particularly with regard to modern, capitalist society. According to Marx, alienation is an especially significant problem of modern work and the modern division of labor in capitalist society. Although Marx's analysis of alienation refers extensively to the economic sphere, Marx goes on to suggest that alienation in economic activity and labor relations cannot help but transform social relations throughout man's life. One ramification of alienation in the economic sphere is a general supersedure of personal uniqueness by impersonality (non-personality, or de-humanization). Alienation in Marx's work needs to be understood together with 'objectification,' and both have a meaning above and beyond any strictly material or economic meaning, comparable to that of 'separation' or distancing, in the general sense that subject and object are divided from the other.

Alienation for Marx is not only an unfortunate aspect of social existence in modern capitalist society, but one that is both exaggerated in capitalist society and unnecessary, given advances in the means of production. Alienation is a central problem of modern capitalist society according to Marx, and his work needs to be understood as, at the most general level, advocating some manner of 'reintegration' (Marx 1978, 84; 1961, 127) or 'reunification' (Ollman 1971, 135). A central insight of Marx's critique of alienation in capitalist society is simply the importance of recognizing "men as both the authors and the actors of their own drama" (Marx 1977, 206). Thus an emphasis on agency is part and parcel of Marx's understanding of modern society, alongside the concern with alienation.

Durkheim also is responsible for the currency of a concept which has been central for the understanding of modernity in sociological theory: 'anomie.' Durkheim's theory of anomie is a key proposition in his sociological analysis of modern society, and he understands modern society to be characterized by a historically unprecedented or even 'pathological' level of anomie. Anomie is defined as 'normlessness' or lack of norms, but we have to recognize, with Olsen, that "such a condition rarely if ever exists in any society" (1965, 37). Durkheim's theory of anomie derives much of its sense from the often implicit comparison to earlier historical periods, featuring greater levels of normative integration, a point which again illustrates the connection between the theory of anomie and the theory of modernity.

Be this as it may, it is clear that anomie is inherently related to *désagrégé*—a state of disintegration, or disaggregated state (Durkheim 1951, 289), or it refers to *dérèglement*—a disordered state or dissoluteness (Durkheim 1951, 253). Under the condition of anomie, according to Durkheim, individuals are only bound together with difficulty, and values lose their meaning or relevance, especially collective or cooperative values.

Durkheim's concern for anomie, or a relative lack of normative regulation, should be understood in the context of his notions of 'mechanical' and 'organic' solidarity. Whereas earlier societies characterized by 'mechanical solidarity' did not face pathological levels of anomie, due to such factors as the similarity of individuals' circumstances and occupations, modern society is characterized by an advanced division of labor, which means that social solidarity must be organic in nature, in other words, must be based on complementarity rather than similarity. Hence modern society faces unique challenges in providing overarching meanings and norms for individuals in diverse walks of life.

Like Marx and Durhkeim, Weber is recognized as a leading theorist of modernity. Weber's position on modernity has been termed 'cultural pessimism.' Weber spoke of the "fate" of modern society, and characterized it by means of concepts such as "bureaucratization," "rationalization," "intellectualization" and the *"disenchantment of the world"* (Weber 1946, 155). According to Weber, the modern West gave birth to a "new form of life" constituted by historical processes of rationalization, and becoming more and more calculating, mechanistic, 'instrumental,' and abstract (Cf. Scaff 1989, 192). The term cultural pessimist has some merit, given Weber's often sobering remarks on modern society. For example, Weber suggests in *The Protestant Ethic and The Spirit of Capitalism*,[1]

> No one any longer knows who will live in this steel-hard casing and whether entirely new prophets or a mighty rebirth of ancient ideas and ideals will stand at the end of this prodigious development. Or, however, if neither, whether a mechanized ossification, embellished with a sort of rigidly compelled sense of self-importance, will arise. Then, indeed, if ossification appears, the saying might be true for the 'last humans' in this long civilizational development: narrow specialists without mind, pleasure-seekers without heart; in its conceit, this nothingness imagines it has climbed to a level of humanity never before attained. (Weber 2001, 124)

Weber's cultural pessimism is arguably counterbalanced, however, by his sensitivity to other aspects of modern society, such as individual autonomy, increasing subjectivity, and freedom, all of which might be appreciated rather than regretted, and all of which are enabled most fully under the circumstances of modern pluralistic society (Kalberg 2000; Smart 1999; Owen 1994; Dallmayr 1994; Maley 1994; Horowitz 1994; Scaff 1989; Seidman 1983a, 1983b; Tiryakian 1981).

With respect to all three of these classical theorists, then, it can be said that they were deeply concerned with cultural as well as structural aspects of modernity, and profoundly ambivalent towards both. Even though they differed significantly about the particulars, all three are generally agreed that the arrival of modern society came with losses as well as gains, and that modern society needed to be understood and evaluated in cultural as well as structural terms. Since the period of classical theory, a concern with modernity has more and more been associated with structural sociology, such as economic sociology, political sociology, and studies of international development or the 'world system.' Many of these analyses have lacked the subtlety of the analyses offered by Marx, Durkheim, and Weber, either because they neglect the role of ideas and values in social life, or because they don't go deeply enough into their subject matter to discover reasons for ambivalence. Sometimes both are true. It is my aim in the following discussion to counter-balance the predominant concern with structural aspects of modernity, to recapture the importance of a cultural or phenomenological understanding of modernity, and to revisit the grounds for ambivalence that come with any deeper understanding of modernity.

PLURALISM

Among the characteristics of modernity, "pluralism" is considered to be one of the most representative characteristics, and it has been explored especially well by Peter Berger. Pluralism, for Berger, refers to the "co-existence with a measure of civic peace of different groups in one society" (Berger 1992, 37). It is reinforced by urbanization, social mobility, market economies, modern communication, technology, and democracy. According to Berger, modernity pluralizes everything in ordinary life, "both institutions and plausibility structures" (Berger 1979, 17).

Moreover, the pluralizing effects of modernity lead to "relativism" (Berger 1973; 1992), because co-existing belief systems challenge each others' credibility. Berger states: "The world view that until now was taken for granted is opened up, very slightly at first, to a glimmer of doubt. This opening has a way of expanding rapidly. The end point may then be a pervasive relativism" (1992, 39). Berger goes on to argue that relativism is a consequence of "cognitive contamination," which is fueled by pluralism (1992). Put differently, the process of pluralization divides the social world into little sectors. It places individuals into situations in which they have to admit or accept unfamiliar or different people, practices, or beliefs.

Pluralization, then, pushes the individual more and more out of the familiar world, to depart into and journey across a fragmented world. Roughly speaking, the modern man continuously alternates temporally, spatially or cognitively through diverse sectors (Berger 1973, 184). Once on this journey, the individual begins to reflect on his familiar world. That is the first step towards suspicion, which leads individuals to begin questioning the familiar world. Pluralism, as Berger and Luckmann nicely sum up, "encourages both skepticism and innovation and is thus inherently subversive of the taken-for-granted reality of the traditional *status quo*" (1966, 125).

Because his journey never ends, modern man is doomed to recurring suspicion. This is the very same phenomenon which the German sociologist Helmut Schelsky calls "*Dauerreflektion*" (permanent reflectiveness) (Zijderveld 1979) and which Anthony Giddens speaks of as "wholesale reflexivity" or "widespread scepticism" (1991, 27). With suspicion, the things (or worlds) taken for granted are put into question, and their ontological status becomes shaken, and then blurred. In other words, pluralism "undermines all certainties" (Berger 1992, 211).[2] What this means can be put quite simply; the pluralized world is filled with discrepancies and lacks all consistency, which is a necessary precondition for certainty. Modernity leads the modern man into a pluralized world characterized by "a multiplicity of incongruencies" (Berger 1997, 202).

Because the modern individual continuously alternates between highly fragmented and discrepant social sectors, he comes to feel that he is hanging around on the outskirts of the world.[3] This feeling results from a lack of attachment. To put this in a different way, in modern society the individual more and more feels he is relegated to a marginal region of the world, inhabiting borderlines between segmented social contexts. Due to his suspicion and continuous migration, modern man finds no place to anchor himself any more, and he wanders here and there, prone to distance himself from societies, social sectors, and individuals.

The concept of 'distance' should be discussed in somewhat greater detail. To do this, we need to refer to Georg Simmel. He formulates his observation on the problem of distance by pointing out the "separation between subject and object" (Simmel 1978, 463). Simmel points out that the process of separation occurs when various options are provided to a man, that is, when a man is located in a pluralistic situation. Simmel states:

> No one speaking his mother tongue naively senses the objective law-like regularities that he has to consult, like

something outside of his own subjectivity, in order to borrow from them resources for expressing his feelings—resources that obey independent norms. Rather, what one wants to express and what one expresses are, in this case, one and the same, and we experience not only our mother tongue but language as such as an independent entity only if we come to know foreign languages. . . . Only where a variety of given styles exists will one detach itself from its content so that its independence and specific significance gives us the freedom to choose between the one or the other. (1978, 462–3)

There can be no doubt that what Simmel calls "*Distanzierung*" (the process of distancing) (1978, 476), is strongly and deeply associated with pluralism. The process of distancing can occur in all the relationships between man and objects, between man and others, and between man and himself. Simmel argues that in premodern times, in which mythology predominated, the distance within all these relationships was much shorter than in modern times. So, it is the modern man who first becomes conscious of distances (Simmel 1978, 475).

For Simmel, "*Fremdheit*" (estrangement or alienation) is another name of the process of distancing (1978, 477). Moreover, Simmel contends that alienation, or an "inner barrier," is in fact necessary for the modern form of life (1978, 477). He suggests:

. . . the jostling crowdedness and the motley disorder of metropolitan communication would simply be unbearable without such psychological distance. Since contemporary urban culture, with its commercial, professional and social intercourse, forces us to be physically close to an enormous number of people, sensitive and nervous modern people would sink completely into despair if the objectification of social relationships did not bring with it an inner boundary and reserve. (Simmel 1978, 477)

If one understands that the process of distancing and alienation leads to an unprecedented quest for the ultimate or authentic meaning of life, it is not surprising that modern times are characterized by "a feeling of tension, expectation and unreleased intense desires—as if in anticipation of what is essential, of the [definition] of the specific meaning and central point of life and things" (Simmel 1978, 481). For modern man, hovering between heterogeneous sections/situations, the process of distancing brings out tensions, frustrations and unsatisfied expectations. This is partly due to uncertainty, as we have mentioned.[4]

But, as Simmel points out, this uncertainty and irregularity is "the unavoidable corollary of freedom" (1978, 338). He goes on to argue that "the manner in which freedom presents itself is irregularity, unpredictability and asymmetry" (1978, 338). Pure freedom, then, is something completely "empty and unbearable" (Simmel 1978, 401). This notion has been expressed by Berger elsewhere; "liberation and alienation are inextricably connected, reverse sides of the same coin of modernity" (1979, 23).[5] Thus, according to Berger, modern man can be described as a "very nervous Prometheus" (1979, 22) or as a man suffering from "a deepening condition of homelessness" (Berger, Berger, and Kellner 1973, 80). It might be argued more broadly that such character-izations of modern man are very similar to that of a permanent wanderer or stranger,[6] since the stranger stays in a marginal ter-rain, distant from the center of society, where he is more likely to feel freedom, but also alienation from the mainstream. To that extent, it is plausible to say that the picture of the stranger applies to modern man very well.

There is, however, a more fundamental dimension of the freedom of modern man as a stranger. Modern man, inhabiting marginal regions, is less likely to take seriously matters of particular sectors; to use Berger's phrase, modern man has more capacity to "take all serious matters with a grain of salt" (1961, 68). This capacity is one of the "fruits of marginality" (Berger 1961, 68). It is even possible that the situation of modern man leads him to an awareness that our whole social reality might be nothing but "artifacts" (Berger 1961, 71). As Berger suggests, what to the premodern man is destiny or fate is for the modern man a possibility or choice, and "destiny is transformed into decision" (1976, 16). Consequently, it is reasonable to surmise that within pluralistic, modern society, modern man expe-riences his actions and others' as a sort of "art" for constructing a particular world as an artifact (Berger 1961, 76).

ABSTRACTION

I have suggested above that abstraction is a major characteristic of modern society, but before discussing the especially abstract nature of modern society, I need to discuss the abstract nature of all societies, of society per se. I do this to avoid the confusion between the abstract nature of society per se and abstraction as one of the major characteristics of modern society.

As Zijderveld (1970, 49) argues, society is abstract by its very nature. This is also recognized by Alfred Schutz (1962; 1964) and Maurice Natanson, especially in their treatments of anonymity and typification, which can be understood as aspects of abstraction. Focusing on Schutz's concept of "typification," Natanson (1986, 22) claims that the concept of "anonymity" is central to Schutz's theory. According to Natanson, Schutz thinks of the social world as the "home of anonymity and of anonymization" (1986, 21). And anonymity refers primarily to "the typified structures of the 'objective' aspect of the social world" (1986, 21).

For Schutz, there is no doubt that the terms 'typification,' 'anonymity,' and 'abstraction' are inseparable, and sometimes even interchangeable.[7] Put differently, they are different aspects of the same phenomenon. But they are also essential for the constitution of the social world; without them, the social world would be impossible (Natanson 1978, 67–8). Natanson acknowledges, for example, that social reality "presupposes and is built upon the principle of anonymization" (1978, 69). Although societies are characterized by varying levels of typification, anonymity and abstraction, every society has them (1978, 69).

With regard to the problem of the self, Natanson presents two arguments concerning anonymity, drawing upon Schutz: anonymity as an essential ground of self (Natanson 1986), and anonymity as a starting point of transcending self (Natanson 1974; 1975; 1977; 1979). Put differently, anonymity is both a mode of socialization of the self as well as a mode of de-socialization (or transcendence) of the self. Even though the two modes appear contradictory, they share the same roots. Natanson elaborates:

> Anonymity might prove to be a clue to selfhood. It would seem that everything in my discussion demonstrates the

opposite: anonymity, whether taken as acts of anonymous agents or aspects of integral acts, whether restricted to roles or referred to the vast realm of signs in the public world, is personless and constitutes a barrier to the fulfillment of individual identity. The apparent contradiction can be resolved in this way: within the essential anonymity of social structure, the individual locates the limits of the typical and comes to recognize what transcends those limits. This recognition is achieved by a self that encounters transcendence, a self that is formed in and through that encounter. (Natanson 1974, 75)

Much more simply, anonymity is one of the essential ingredients for constituting the self. To that extent, anonymity has a positive effect on the individual, despite the conventional, commonsensible, pessimistic critique of anonymity. If we bring together Schutz's, Natanson's, and Zijderveld's accounts, it would seem that anonymity and abstraction are necessary, for premodern as well as modern society. Abstraction, anonymity and typification allow for unreflective–repetitive behaviors, and things taken for granted, which are necessary as a base for the constitution of self as well as a transcendence of it.

Taking up the problem of the degree of anonymity, however, the anonymity of modern times appears to be extreme. Anonymity and abstraction are exaggerated and excessive in modern society. I would like to call this an explosion of anonymity and abstraction, in which these have outgrown their original, positive roles.

Because of the explosion of anonymity and abstraction, modern man has great difficulty identifying the basic grounds for constituting and maintaining his self, and identifying what would be a basis for transcending it. This has a direct relation to modern man's crisis of identity. The modern turmoil, resulting mainly from the disintegration of the stock of knowledge, as Schutz puts it (1964, 120), leads modern man into a travail of permanent reflection. To that extent, when Zijderveld speaks of abstract society, he means essentially the same process that Arnold Gehlen refers to as de-institutionalization,[8] since both require continuous reflection.

Abstraction (or anonymity) is a shelter where the self can be fostered, raised, and hidden. However, with modernization, the level of abstraction reaches its summit. As a consequence, modern man suffers from a confusion about his external life, and turns inward in a process of subjectivization. If we admit Natanson's suggestion that "anonymity replaces inwardness" (1986, 128), we can perhaps revise it to indicate that in modern society a high degree of anonymity (or abstraction) fails to replace inwardness, but is accompanied by a return to inwardness.

Following from the above analysis, the modern world can be described as a world of strangers. Because modern society is a world of strangers, it must be essentially abstract. What does this mean, that modern society is essentially abstract? Zijderveld provides us with a useful illustration of the abstraction of modern society.

According to Zijderveld, while modern society becomes more and more pluralized, society loses much of its "existential concreteness" (1970, 49). The loss of existential concreteness means the abstraction of society. An abstract society becomes unable to provide man with a "clear awareness of his identity and reality" (1970, 48).[9] He goes on to argue that modern society has become abstract in "the experience and consciousness of man" (1970, 49). In other words, in the abstract society of the modern world, man does not "live society" any more, but "faces it" as abstract, vague, and opaque (1970, 49). As we have shown above, in the process of modernization, realities become more and more fragmented due to pluralization and specialization. Moreover, the segmented sectors of modern society are often inconsistent with, contradictory to, or distant from each other. In this sense, society fails to provide the individual with one coherent system of meanings.

Abstraction grows not only with pluralization, but also with geographic distance, size of society, and social distance (Zijderveld 1970, 52–5). W. I. Thomas forwards a similar observation, by pointing out the vagueness of the modern world in his *The Unadjusted Girl* (1967):

> The definition of the situation is equivalent to the determination of the vague. In the Russian mire and the American rural community of fifty years ago nothing was left vague, all was defined. But in the general world movement to which I have referred, connected with free

communication in space and free communication of thought, not only particular situations but the most general situations have become vague. (81–2)

While illustrating the phenomenon of the separation of space from place in modern times, Giddens (1990) suggests an understanding like that of Zijderveld and Thomas, with his idea of an "empty dimension" (1990, 20), including the "emptying of time and space" (1990, 18), and appearing to have nothing to do with any given situation or face-to-face interaction. It goes well beyond that. And it is very anonymous and abstract (1990, 18–21). According to Giddens, the empty dimension is characterized by institutions which are "disembedded," 'lifted out' of particular-local contexts of presence (1990, 21). These disembedded institutions are characterized by a high degree of standardization and ambiguity.

Within a similar context, Simmel also conceives of the modern world as an impersonal, objective and anonymous one (1950b; 1978). For Simmel, the modern world is alienated, due to the high degree of objectification[10] and abstraction. He formulates: "The sense of being oppressed by the externalities of modern life is not only the consequence but also the cause of the fact that they confront us as autonomous objects. What is distressing is that we are basically indifferent to those numerous objects that swarm around us, and this is for reasons specific to a money economy: their impersonal origin and easy replaceability" (Simmel 1978, 460).

As Zijderveld observes, when modern man tries to understand society in order to pursue the meaning and authenticity of his life, modern society immediately "evaporates" into "an awareness of loss of meaning and reality" (Zijderveld 1970, 49–50).

More specifically, what characteristics are observable in the abstract, modern society? In his *On Clichés* (1979), Zijderveld claims that abstract, modern society is characterized by a loss of "uniqueness," and the "supersedure of meaning by function." Drawing upon Walter Benjamin's notion of the "decline of aura,"[11] and Helmut Schelsky's theories of the levelling[12] of modern society (1965), Zijderveld argues that modern society is an abstract, "cliché-genic" society (1979, 26). He focuses on the use of language in everyday modern life, and observes that with functional exchange replacing meaning in language use, the use of clichés becomes more and more frequent. Cliché-genic society, therefore, emphasizes functionality rather than uniqueness, and becomes more and more standardized and leveled.

However, if we look more carefully, we can see that clichés are necessary in modern society. My point is that, in the midst of an ambiguous, unpredictable, abstract world, which no longer provides modern man with stable guidance and meaning, the social relationships between modern individuals are endangered.[13] Clichés have been the most important conduits for behavior, allowing modern individuals to connect smoothly with each other without any hassles. If one understands this, it is not surprising why Zijderveld considers clichés to be "beacons" in a world of vagueness, instability and uncertainty (1979, 46). By the same token, the following insight from Hanna Arendt is relevant and suggestive; after observing the trial of Eichmann in Jerusalem, Arendt noted: "Clichés, stock phrases, adherence to conventional, standardized codes of expression and conduct have the socially recognized *function of protecting* us against reality, that is, against the claim on our thinking attention which all events and facts arouse by virtue of their existence. If we were responsive to this claim all the time, we would soon be exhausted" (Arendt 1971, 418; emphasis added).

To use a metaphor, a layman knows nothing about the mechanics of a jumbo jet—it is completely abstract. However, if he has a boarding ticket, he can easily board the plane and fly where he wants to go, without his ignorance causing any inconvenience. Clichés in modern times play a role like the boarding ticket.

Moreover, since clichés as symbolic tokens[14] provide modern man with "some degree of clarity, stability and certainty," they can be considered as the most important "institution" in modern society (Zijderveld 1979, 72). Zijderveld suggests that "clichés resemble institutions. . . . In fact, we could view clichés as micro-institutions, while the institutions of modernized society tend to grow into macro-clichés" (1979, 17).

It is easy to explain why clichés have developed into institutions: modernity undermines certainty. Everything is put into doubt. However, since the human mind "abhors uncertainty" (Berger 1990, 45), modern man feels uncertainty as a burden and pain. Therefore, modern man seeks to avoid it. If traditional certainties in social order and institutions, and religious certainties, are no longer available to modern man, he has to find alternative certainties (or order), like the ones found by the characters in Robert Musil's novel *The Man Without Qualities* (1996), such as music or mathematics.[15] Unfortunately, however, clichés have poignant limitations as alternative institutions. They, too, are inherently rooted in the ambiguity and abstraction of modern society. The clarity, stability, and certainty clichés provide are "artificial" (Zijderveld 1979, 47), and the comfort they give is nothing but a "temporal rest" (Zijderveld 1979, 49).

Despite the limit of clichés, however, it is still plausible to argue that for modern life, in which uncertainty leads to permanent reflection, clichés play a significant role in soothing, stabilizing, or mitigating the increasing tensions and burdens of modern man.[16] Their "repetitiveness" allows some degree of relief from permanent reflection (Zijderveld 1979, 65).

Because modern society emphasizes functional exchange, it tends to forget its tradition and history. This 'a-historical tendency' leads to the 'contingency' or 'temporality' of modern social existence.[17] Zijderveld describes this condition as the total absence of permanence (1979, 39–44). This absence of permanence has deep affinities with the "disposability of objects" in modern society (Zijderveld, 1979, 35). That is, in modern society, because of the pervasive notion that nothing is fixed, permanent and eternal,[18] there is the feeling everything is replaceable, even human beings.[19]

In sum, abstraction, the decline of aura (or uniqueness), the emphasis on functional exchange, and the disposability and replaceability of objects are different aspects of the same phenomenon.

But abstraction is not restricted to society: it is true of people as well.[20] There is no less abstraction with individuals than there is with society. Abstraction impinges rapidly and unseen on the identity of the individual. It undermines to some degree his identity and self-concept.

How is this possible? First of all, in abstract society, personal face-to-face relations are likely to have been replaced by anonymous relations between social roles. To that extent, much of modern society appears to consist of socially "dead" places. For instance, as Zijderveld suggests, a supermarket in a metropolitan region is a socially dead place because of its emphasis on function and role rather than personality (1979, 32). Individuals tend to be perceived or treated as abstract or anonymous beings, non-personalities who are objectified and marginal (Simmel 1978, 297; 1950a; 1950b) like "a guest in a hotel room". In other words, the picture of a person as a concrete being with personal qualities disappears, and the modern individual becomes a stranger, a non-person without qualities. Like the abstraction of society, the tendency to neglect personal qualities illustrates modern man's emphasis on functionality or utility rather than uniqueness. Put differently, in abstract society, the uniqueness of individuals loses its priority in social relations, and instead, functional exchange value prevails. Simmel suggests that the modern personality: ". . . is almost completely destroyed under the conditions of a money economy. The deliveryman, the money-lender, the worker, upon whom we are dependent do not operate as personalities because they enter into a relationship only by virtue of a single activity such as the delivery of goods, the lending of money, and because their other qualities, which alone would give them a personality, are missing" (1978, 296).

Simmel (1978, 389) goes on to point out the decrease of "*Vornehmlichkeit*" (distinction), which he considers to be a "*Persönlichkeitsideal*" (personal ideal), due to the development of a money economy in modern times. The distinguished person, according to him, is the very person who "completely reserves his personality," and distinction is a "quite unique combination of senses of differences that are based upon and yet reject any comparison at all" (Simmel 1978, 390). Yet, the more functional exchange, like economic exchange, prevails in society, the less distinction can be valued and appreciated in men and objects (Simmel 1978, 391). Put differently, abstract modern society is populated by individuals who have lost their distinction, beings without qualities.[21] This phenomenon can easily be interpreted, with Simmel, as "degradation" (1978, 390), and "lack of character" (1978, 432), and with Berger, as "the obsolescence of the concept of honor" (1970b).

Modern individuals, as beings without qualities, are not likely to be stable, but likely to choose or experience many changes. As Simmel aptly notes, modern man has a "penchant for change (*Variabilität*)" (1978, 462). With regard to this tendency, Berger suggests that the "man without qualities is, at the same time, the man of possibility . . . The possibility of alteration" (1970a, 230–1). Put differently, modern man can be described as a being-in-alteration (Cf. Berger 1992, 114; 1961; 1966).[22] It would appear that modern man is more, and more easily, absorbed with things, and also discards these more, and more easily, than pre–modern man. Modern man's words, thoughts, emotions and actions become rather "unreliable and unpredictable" (Zijderveld 1979, 49). Therefore, modern man's behaviors often seem to be capricious, and on the spur of the moment, and thus inherently temporal and contingent.[23]

However, this erratic nature of modern man's behavior can also be viewed as an attempt to overcome or escape "ennui or boredom,"[24] which seem endemic to modern society. To that extent, the contingency or temporality of modern life is closely related to the problem of boredom. Modern man, as a man with possibilities of alteration, is able to choose among a great variety of options. But what is distressing is that his fate is to be alone, choosing from a morass of choices over his whole life. Modern man can be seen to be tormented, and possibly depressed by endless choices. It is safe to hypothesize that the life of choices begins with nervousness, and ends with boredom. The temporality and contingency of modern life, which always requires modern man to make decisions, is enough to suffocate him with tensions and boredom. And then, modern man reacts to boredom with unpredictable or erratic behaviors again and again, which are characterized by temporality or contingency *in nucleo.* Thus temporality and boredom are engaged in a ceaseless feedback process. Consequently, modern man feels helplessly caught up in a life that is empty and void. With regard to this, we can quote the apt characterization of modern man's volatility by Simmel:

> The lack of something definite at the center of the soul impels us to search for momentary satisfaction in ever-new stimulations, sensations and external activities, thus it is that we become entangled in the instability and helplessness that manifests itself as the tumult of the metropolis, as the mania for travelling, as the wild pursuit of competition and as the typically modern disloy-

alty with regard to taste, style, options and personal relationships. (1978, 484)

The replaceability and disposability of human beings, and the emphasis on functional exchange mentioned above, are the clearest illustrations of the unpredictability, contingency, and temporality of modern man life.[25]

By the very nature of contingency, modern man can also be understood as disconnected from his past. That is, like modern society, modern man as an abstract being is an a–historical being, without tradition. As Christopher Lasch (1980; 1985) argues, with modern man there is "loss of historical continuity" in the sense of meaningfully belonging to a succession of generations going back into the past. Zijderveld also notes a relationship between an "anti-institutional mood" and the "a-historical abodes of modern man's subjectivism" (1972; 1979).

The picture of modern man invoked here is a somewhat pessimistic, grim and gloomy image of the modern individual, who appears to be much like a cog in a huge machine. This image might be appropriate, because it illustrates the alienation of modern man. Yet, this is not the whole story of the abstraction of modern man and society. It would be quite possible to approach the problem of the abstraction of modernity from a totally different perspective, one emphasizing freedom.

Just as pluralism in modern society leads to the coincidence of freedom and alienation, abstraction too provides for both freedom and alienation. First of all, modern man never completely becomes a cog in the machine. Modern man is continuously changing his roles, "like the jackets of a wardrobe," and consequently he cannot "maintain the bond between himself and the institutions of his society" (Zijderveld 1970, 130). Whereas pre-modern man could not freely and realistically imagine this possibility, modern man can always—and sometimes must—change roles substantially and rapidly.[26] A permanent or perfect match between man and his roles is therefore only a memory or legend. There is, however, a more fundamental reason why abstraction allows the modern man freedom. Non-personality, anonymity and abstraction essentially guarantee freedom by their very nature. They are the home of freedom; whereas personal relations bring obligations and constraints, abstract and anonymous relations bring freedom. Therefore, anonymity is freedom as well as alienation. Generally speaking, however, when we speak of anonymity, we tend to focus on just the latter. I believe that is narrow and one-sided.

Therefore, the desirable company for modern man, as Simmel (1978, 227) sharply observes, is the person "completely indifferent to us, engaged neither for us (friends) nor against us (enemies)," who is, in other words, anonymous. Simmel goes on to claim that freedom increases with objectivization and depersonalization (1978, 303). Abstraction, objectivization, depersonalization and anonymity reach their peak when the world is conceived as a "system of numbers" (Simmel 1978, 444) instead of as qualitatively distinct men and events. Again, viewed with a more jaundiced eye, the picture is a negative one in which all distinctions and characteristics of modern man are erased by abstraction. However, viewed positively, it is of much greater interest for us that abstraction has a moral character: it implies equality. That is, abstraction results in a "democratic levelling where everyone counts as one and no one counts for more than one" (Simmel 1978, 444). Regardless of race, ethnicity, class, age, gender, or nationality, no one stands above or beneath others. Put differently, equality can be considered as a freedom from the constraints of particular, personal categories.

In sum, the process of liberation, as Simmel (1978, 404) points out, is driven by the growing abstraction of modern society. The modern world is one of unprecedented freedom for modern man. Without stable characteristics or qualities, modern man comes and goes between diverse sectors of the world, treating others and treated by others as the incumbent of several abstract and anonymous categories (or social roles), but inwardly denying that these categories are essential to others or himself. After all, he tends to emphasize the fact that we are all human beings whenever he tries to connect to others, as if he notices the fictitiousness of social roles. He therefore experiences emptiness, loneliness, and anxiety, but at the same time, freedom. In a similar vein, Fromm writes in *Escape from Freedom*:

> The individual is freed from the bondage of economic and political ties. He also gains in positive freedom by

the active and independent role which he has to play in the new system. But simultaneously he is freed from those ties which used to give him security and a feeling of belonging. . . . By losing his fixed place in a closed world man loses the answer to the meaning of his life; the result is that doubt has befallen him concerning himself and the aim of life...he is free—that is, he is alone, isolated, threatened from all sides . . . and also having lost the sense of unity with men and the universe, he is overwhelmed with a sense of his individual nothingness and helplessness. Paradise is lost for good, the individual stands alone and faces the world. . . . The new freedom is bound to *create* a deep feeling of insecurity, powerlessness, doubt, aloneness, and anxiety. (Fromm 1941, 62–3)

Similarly, Charles Taylor suggests:

. . . full freedom would be situationless. And by the same token, empty. Complete freedom would be a void in which nothing would be worth doing, nothing would deserve to count for anything. The self which has arrived at freedom by setting aside all external obstacles and impingements is characterless, and hence without defined purpose, however much this is hidden by such seemingly positive terms as 'rationality' or 'creativity'. These are ultimately quite indeterminate as criteria for human action or mode of life. (Taylor 1975, 561)

Given these sensibilities, it should not be surprising that the occasional social theorist, such as Fromm (1941), discusses the possibility that the modern individual might want to escape from the new form of freedom present in modern society.

Because modern man is not anchored, but free-floating, without any destination, he conceives of roles as depending upon places and time; he continuously questions assignments of roles and the corresponding treatments and justifications, and ultimately departs to trace his true self (identity). As Simmel states, modern man is often characterized by an "insecure personality, which can hardly be pinned down and placed" because his "mobility and versatility" saves him from committing himself in any situation (1978, 433). It can therefore be argued that for modern man "*Schlauheit* (Shrewdness)" (Simmel 1978, 433)—or, what Zijderveld (1979, 34) calls the "art of performing itself" is conceived not just as a way of behaving, but rather a sort of fate.

Before concluding this discussion, it should be noted that Schutz's and Zijderveld's theories of abstraction do diverge in some respects. When Schutz speaks of abstraction or anonymity, they refer to sediments of meanings created through the "repeated action" (Schutz 1961, 20–21) of human beings. Abstraction, for Schutz, can therefore coexist with unreflectiveness. There is a terrain of freedom or relief which is rooted upon an unreflectiveness made possible by abstraction. By contrast, when Zijderveld refers to the abstraction of modern society, he means an excessive degree of abstraction. It is no longer an abstraction which provides for stable meanings, but which is characterized by permanent reflection, ambiguity, vagueness, autonomy, indifference, and remoteness. In Zijderveld's case, freedom is based upon an abstract uncertainty, in the sense that uncertainty is accompanied by a sense of possibility and the capability of making a decision.

Whatever the differences, what is important here is that both Schutz's and Zijderveld's accounts of abstraction see it as allowing for freedom (or transcendence).

SOME OTHER CHARACTERISTICS OF MODERNITY

The two major characteristics of modernity discussed above, pluralism and abstraction, are accompanied by additional features, including the mutual autonomization of the institutional order and man, the weakening of roles and the growth of individualism, and regression into the *hic et nunc* ('here and now').

The Mutual Autonomization of the Institutional Order and Man

Due to the pluralism and abstraction of modern society, man and society are growing more and more autonomous from each other. Thomas Luckmann has called this "the discrepancy between the subjective autonomy of the individual and the objective autonomy of the social institution" (1967, 97). Consequently, the values, meanings, motives and norms of modern society no longer bind individuals, but are free-floating (Zijderveld 1970; 1979). In his *The Abstract Society*, Zijderveld formulates:

> Contemporary society exhibits a disparity between the individual and the institutional structures of his society. The latter have the tendency to grow independent and to exist for their own sake. The individual, on the other hand, seems to take the opposite road, to withdraw from the public sphere into his private world and grow increasingly autonomous, often in a rather subjectivistic way. (1970, 128)

Although Daniel Bell makes no direct efforts to address this issue, I can think of no more cogent summation than his suggestion that the modern nation-state has become "too small for the big problems of life, and too big for the small problems of life" (1967, 82).

Consequently, modern man, who is no longer anchored in society, can be seen as free-floating (Zijderveld 1979, 41). That is, even though there is a high degree of reification, reified structures don't seriously influence, bind, or constrain modern man. So the conventional critique which sees reification or society as constraining is much too narrow. The mutual autonomization of society and man brings with it an extreme reification, connected to the extreme abstraction of modern society, mentioned above. As with abstraction, extreme levels of reification have the counter–intuitive effect of providing freedom for modern man.

The mutual autonomization of modern man and society, driven by growing levels of abstraction, is accelerated by the other characteristics of modern life, including the "anti–institutional mood" (Zijderveld, 1972), the process of "de-institutionalization" and "subjectivization" (Gehlen 1956; 1980), and the "democratisation of personal life" (Giddens 1992, 182). According to Gehlen, de-institutionalization (i.e. when the institutional order loses meaning, influence and reality) results in the increased importance of the realm of subjectivity, a process Gehlen has called "subjectivization" (1956; 1980). Put differently, modern society brings about a "far-reaching reality-loss on the part of the institutional order" (Berger 1974, 173). Gehlen goes on to argue that in modern times, due to specialization and abstraction, society no longer possesses the cultural capacity to provide modern man with a coherent world-view. Then, instead of seeking certainty or meaning from the external-institutional order, modern man begins to turn his eyes inward.[27] Concomitantly, there is a "reality-gain of subjectivity" (Berger 1974, 174). I would like to quote at length Luckmann's succinct description of the mutual autonomization of self and the resulting subjectivization:

> In this respect modern society differs not only from primitive societies, but also from traditional pre-industrial cultures. The world view—no longer firmly based on the social structure—now consists of a supply of items from which individuals may add on to the basic inventory that was built up in primary socialization. No particular version of the world view is strictly obligatory or inescapably predetermined by the social structure. Personal identity is not a matter of the sociohistoric a priori to quite the same extent as in other forms of society. Personal identity of course continues to emerge from social processes, but the social *production* of cohesive models of personal identity is largely abandoned by the social system. The production of personal identity thus increasingly becomes the business of the most private *petit entrepreneur*, the human individual. (Luckmann 1987, 379–80)

The Weakening of Roles and the Growth of Individualism

In Adam Seligman's *The Problem of Trust* (1997), he notes that modern man is prone to be somewhat distanced from all his social roles. In other words, modern man dodges the roles which society assigns to him.[28]

The above traits of modern man are closely related to two specific features of modern society: *the crisis of socialization* and *the emergence of trust*. These must be addressed now.

Generally speaking, in all societies, socialization is always incomplete (Berger and Luckmann 1966). In other words, a complete socialization is an impossible feat. Every society has difficulty in socializing its members, since socialization is by nature not a one-directional process, but a bargaining process between society and its members (Berger 1974, 163). But the difficulty of socialization seems to reach its peak in modern society. In modern society the bargaining process of socialization is disrupted. Disruption results from the fact that for the individual man, the counterpart in the bargaining process is vague, due to the abstraction of society, and due to the discrepancies or contradictions within the contents of what is taught in socialization, due to pluralization. For instance, one of the key tasks of socialization is the allocation and assignment of role or identity to the individual. However, in the modern condition, as we have discussed briefly above, the individual is relatively free from any roles or identities which society assigns. Berger calls this the "open-endedness of modern identity," and the "convertible quality of modern identity" (Berger 1974, 173). Put differently, modern man, as the man without qualities or the man of possibility, is open to an endless "self-transformation" (Berger 1970, 231).

Luckmann provides similar arguments:

Social roles which are necessary structural elements of all societies inevitably become anonymous in some measure. It hardly needs to be stressed that social roles are a necessary constituent of modern industrial societies. But when most social roles become highly anonymous and thereby depersonalized, the individual's personal identity is no longer clearly shaped by the social order in which he lives. (1987, 378)

I would describe this incapacity of modern society as the demoralization or impotence of social order. Social order can no longer firmly or strictly assign identities to man, since identities are experienced as "ever-changing, opaque, unsafe—in the final case, as devoid of reality" (Berger 1974, 173).

This issue can be examined with regard to abstraction. Here I would like to relate modern man's escape from his roles to Jean-Paul Sartre's concept of 'bad faith' (Sartre 1956). If we may elaborate upon Sartre's concept, bad faith can be paraphrased, *mutatis mutandis*, as taking for granted the given world and the "moral or social alibi"[29] assigned by the world. With a perfect case of bad faith, man truly, really, simply, naïvely, fully, and literally identifies himself with roles given by society, and takes these for granted. If we understand bad faith like this, then it is very hard to find any bad faith in modern society. It is no exaggeration to say that modern man is too smart to take an assigned identity for granted, so he would appear to be free of bad faith. Rather, modern man appears to be much more 'authentic'[30] in the sense that he resists social roles and seeks his "true self" (Berger 1973, 82).

The reason why modern man is free of bad faith and strives for authenticity can be clearly stated: modernity exposes everything to unprecedented doubts. All things previously taken for granted are thrown into question. The certainty of the world is undermined. Doubt also undermines role-taking. Bad faith, because it is founded upon taking things for granted, becomes more and more difficult. To give a specific example, religion has traditionally been a key provider of moral alibis and has played a most important role in constituting bad faith, as Berger (1971) indicates. But religion too, is no longer taken for granted.[31] Therefore, one can say that the more questions, suspicion and reflection there is, the less bad faith occurs.

The increase of freedom in modernity is also related to the decrease in bad faith. If we allow that bad faith is inversely related with freedom,[32] the unprecedented freedom of modern life would seem to prevent the development of bad faith. Indeed, modern man is bent on eluding all roles which would be "pinned to his chest" (Berger 1974, 163). Concomitantly, modern man experiences a peculiar "weightlessness"[33] of the self, and experiences a feeling of "vertigo" (Berger 1973, 86).

But of course, there are things taken for granted in every society, modern society included. And because bad faith is possible whenever there are things taken for granted, as Berger points out, "it is most difficult to imagine any society not containing the possibility of bad faith" (1961, 92–3). But Berger goes further, suggesting that "perhaps bad faith is one of the essential ingredients of being human" (1961, 92–3). Man can even be said to need bad faith (Berger 1961, 125), since it provides individuals with comfort and "the warm feeling of being at home that a horse has in its stable" (Berger 1970, 216). This is acknowledged by Natanson as well:

> Bad Faith amounts to the freezing of temporality, the denial of openness and flexibility of the present as a basis for the reconstruction of the past no less than as a foundation for assessing and selecting lines for advance to the future. The temporality of the individual in Bad Faith is sealed in and abandoned to fixation, a permanent image, settled and secure, with all danger of vitality gutted out. (1970a, 91)

Thus, one is almost tempted to say that bad faith is not actually bad.[34] If, however, one grants that bad faith is always possible, and that bad faith is not necessarily bad, then perhaps modern society is characterized by a modified form of bad faith. In modern society it is hard to see bad faith in the traditional naïve mode, but one can see a "shrewd bad faith," so to speak—such as the use of alibis as excuses for conduct.

Social entities such as the social system, social structure, social order, etc., remain vague, somewhat unreal, and thus have little to do with modern man any more. Yet, when modern man needs to explain, justify, or give an excuse, social entities can be invoked, used, manipulated, and finally, embodied as if they were still quite real. Put differently, in such situations, when the abstract social system, social institutions, structures and order are embodied and incarnated, bad faith can be seen to be working in a modified way.

Briefly speaking, pre-modern man lived in and through bad faith, and was hardly aware of it. Thus, the age of bad faith was relatively long. By contrast, modern man recognizes bad faith and avoids it in its traditional form, or at most manipulates it. Instances of bad faith are now tremendously short, momentary, and temporary. The modified bad faith of modern man is much more liberating than constraining. To that extent, we can say that a modified bad faith contributes to modern man's freedom from his social roles.

Modern man is reducible to none of his roles—spousal, political, occupational, racial, ethnic, life-stage, gender, or any other (Seligman 1997, 57). How is this freedom from roles achieved?

To begin with, despite common conceptions, modern man is free even while he is role-playing or role-taking.[35] This is made possible by three factors. First, there is a possibility of transcendence[36] enabled by the stability and repetitiveness of roles and role-taking. Second, there is relief from the burden of endless reflection, invention, and modification which characterizes life outside of roles. Third, there is a freedom which comes with the anonymity and abstraction of roles. But modern man not only achieves freedom within roles—he can also achieve freedom by abandoning roles. So there is freedom in modern man's willingness to take on roles, and freedom in his reluctance to take on roles.

After all, modern man feels a kind of freedom and transcendence all the time. He sometimes even becomes aware that he is taking a role. That is, modern man can conceive of his role-taking as simply acting, restricted only by his own will.

In his *The Problem of Trust*, Seligman points out that the modern situation leads to 'opaqueness' in social relations.[37] This means that individuals can no longer accurately predict others' intentions and calculations in light of their roles, since in modern society, as we have already discussed, individuals seem to be distanced from all social roles. Under this condition, trust can increase, because trust can only be placed in "something beyond the role, something irreducible to the role's fulfillment" (Seligman 1977, 55). But in modernity, trust is insecure, uncertain, and fragile. By contrast, in pre-modern times, when individuals were inseparable from their roles, social relations were characterized by confidence, which was stable, secure, and certain (Seligman 1977).

Trust, therefore, appears to be inherently bound up with unpredictability, uncertainty, contingency, and temporality (Giddens 1990, 145). Because these all foster freedom, trust is closely related to the freedom of modern man. But modern individuals' awareness of freedom is an awareness of the freedom of others as well as their own. Trust in others is therefore inseparable from the awareness of others' freedom. Peter Johnson suggests that "to speak then of the origins of trust is to describe the variety of ways in which agents become conscious of the freedom of others" (1993, 79). Regardless of what others do, what roles they take on, or what categories they fall into, they come to be conceived as human beings, in other words, just people. This tendency is similar to the pursuit of "pure relationships" discussed by Giddens (1991, 88). Giddens also suggests that pure relationships presuppose equality and democratization (1992, 183, 185). In this regard, Benjamin Nelson argues: "It is a tragedy of modern history that the expansion of the area of the moral community has ordinarily been gained through the sacrifice of the intensity of the moral bond, or . . . that all men have been becoming brothers by becoming equally others" (1969, 136).

This tendency of considering others as human beings per se, rather than as occupants of their roles, certainly results from the pluralism and abstraction of modern society. As we have seen earlier, pluralism brings with it a high level of role segmentation, and then discrepancies between roles become more frequent. As a result, roles are experienced as incoherent, abstract, vague, and finally, powerless and useless. Modern man takes this into account when he considers others. Consequently, modern man is prone to rely more and more upon the basic humanity of others, rather than their superficial roles. But it is also true that modern man's notion of humanity is highly abstract and vague.

Be this as it may, there is no doubt that the tendency to look beyond roles does have a very close relationship with the development of individualism. With regard to this, Rose Laub Coser's comments are suggestive:

> As role expectations are more diffuse, and as attitudes are the basis for their allocation and judgement, more decisions are left to the individual. . . . Individualism thrives under conditions of role-set complexity because such conditions make it possible for individuals to decide whether or not to involve their internal dispositions when they try to conform to the demands of some role partners. (1991, 92–93)

Thus individualism grows with the decline of the power of roles. The emergence of individualism in modern society has also been noted by Fromm. He observes the increased individualism of modern times, comparing it to pre-modern society. He remarks, for example:

Everybody in the earlier period was chained to his role in the social order. . . . But although a person was not free in the modern sense, neither was he alone and isolated. In having a distinct, unchangeable, and unquestionable place in the social world from the moment of birth, man was rooted in a structuralized whole, and thus life had a meaning which left no place, and no need, for doubt. A person was identical with his role in society; he was a peasant, an artisan, a knight, and not an *individual* who *happened* to have this or that occupation. . . . The result of this progressive destruction of the medieval social structure was the emergence of the individual in the modern sense. (Fromm 1941, 41–5; emphasis in original)

The Regression into the hic et nunc (Here and Now)

Neither the consciousness nor the activity of humans is fixed by nature. Plessner and Gehlen call this quality "world openness *(Weltoffenheit)*." They suggest that while animals are "closed" beings, "openness" is a "typical human phenomenon" (Gehlen 1988, 181).[38] Drawing from Plessner, Gehlen notes the following: "Man can create a gulf between himself and his experiences; he exists on both sides of the gulf, tied to the body and tied to the soul, but at the same time he exists nowhere; he is beyond space and time and is therefore human" (1988, 252). Put differently, human being is being-in-transcendence, not merely a being-in-the *hic et nunc* (here and now), whereas animals exist only in the *hic et nunc*.

Modern man, however, appears to live only in the *hic et nunc*, like animals.[39] It appears that modern man only understands what is in the *hic et nunc*. His identity, meaning, motives, and world are only clear to him in the context of the *hic et nunc*. Anything beyond the *hic et nunc* is blurred and obscure. He therefore emphasizes and adheres more and more to the *hic et nunc*.

Paradoxically, man's interest in taking advantage of his 'world openness,' his natural inclination for exploration or eccentricity,[40] declines in modernity, when advanced technology and engineering give him unprecedented freedom and opportunities.[41] As we have already mentioned above, the close relationship of time and space has been destroyed.[42] The previously cozy *Umwelt* has therefore expanded without limits,[43] bringing with it the possibility of a radical transcendence of the *hic et nunc*. But this tremendous freedom is experienced as vagueness and uncertainty and modern man becomes bewildered. Put simply, this is an unbearable burden for modern man. Nothing is clear to him, and he begins to seek clarity and certainty. He has to literally start all over again, to define everything around him again every day, every moment. It is an endless effort. For modern man, therefore, certainty appears to be available only in the *hic et nunc*, and he therefore returns to it for protection.

Modern man's search for the self illustrates the emphasis on the *hic et nunc*. As Berger aptly indicates, the question 'who am I?' can be "answered only *hic et nunc*" (Berger 1974, 172). Similarly, Luckmann points out that in the formation of personal identity, modern man tends not to go beyond the *hic et nunc* of "reciprocal mirroring" with those co-present (Luckmann 1987, 373). Following Gehlen, Luckmann argues that the full development of personal identity actually presupposes the individual's detachment from the *hic et nunc* (1987, 368). For Luckmann, therefore, the *hic et nunc* of "reciprocal mirroring" is a "necessary condition but not a sufficient condition" for the full development of personal identity (1987, 373). Unfortunately, in modern times there is "no common social reality" (1987, 379), so personal identity is formed only in the *hic et nunc*. Under modern circumstances, therefore, there is "no socially produced stable structure of personal identity" (1987, 379).

In conclusion, due to the abstraction, ambiguity and the dislocation of time and space in modernity, everything is opaque and obscure to modern man except in his *hic et nunc*. Only when self and others are copresent can people achieve clarity about self, others, and the world. Even though the clarity is temporal, superficial, shallow, and vague, modern man is inclined to cling to the moment. Boden and Molotch (1994) call this tendency "compulsion toward proximity." They note the central necessity of copresent interaction in modern society as follows:

> Features of copresent interaction make it fundamental
> to social order, both local and global. The immediacy

and inherent indexicality of all human existence means that the fine, fleeting, yet essentially social moments of everyday life anchor and articulate the modern macro-order. Through the trust, commitment, and detailed understandings made possible in situations of copresence the essential space-time distantiation of modern society is achieved. (Boden and Molotch 1994, 277)

Put differently, for Boden and Molotch, the *hic et nunc* of copresence is necessary for the existence of macro phenomena.

Furthermore, the emphasis on the *hic et nunc* is deeply related to the remarkable shift in attention from personal qualities or characteristics to performance or skills. Since one pays much attention to the *hic et nunc*, there is a stress on skills to fit particular situations, especially skills designed to maintain these situations. In the modern situation 'the art of performance' becomes more emphasized, even essential in ordinary life. It is the very same phenomenon that Berger calls the "process of ploying and one-upmanship" (1961), and what Zijderveld names the "art of performing" (1979, 34), and what Natanson calls the "art of daily life" (1970, 87).

Thus far we have examined several characteristics of modernity. To sum up, the above analysis suggests the following picture: Primitive man lived in a tiny cave in order to avoid such things as severe weather or wild animals.[44] He felt comfortable and at home. The walls and ceiling of the cave were close by, so the cave was a warm and cozy shelter for him. By contrast, modern man lives in a giant stadium. It is hard to see its ceiling and walls, and there is no coziness and comfort. Rather, it is extremely immense and desolate. It is colorless, odorless, faceless, abstract, vague, and, finally, meaningless. When this is realized, insecurity creeps over modern man. His situation resembles that of pre-modern man in the wilderness, before finding shelter in a cave. That is, man is once again in the teeth of tremendous uncertainty.

It will be the task of the following chapters to scrutinize the manner in which the above understanding of modern man and society is reflected in the theories of Parsons, Goffman, and Garfinkel.

2

TALCOTT PARSONS

The aim of this chapter is to outline the understanding of modernity in Parsons's theory of social order and human agency.

SOCIAL ORDER

In order to uncover Parsons's understanding of social order, we have to begin with Parsons's epistemology and conception of the nature of theory. In other words, we can grasp Parsons's view of social order by looking at his view of theory itself.

Social Order as Theoretical Construction

I begin by discussing the "Kantian problem" and the "Weberian problem," which greatly influenced the development of Parsons's notion of social order (Parsons 1967, 148). Briefly speaking, Parsons, unlike Karl Marx, approaches the problem of order in terms of non–material conditions. To that extent, Parsons's approach falls within the Kantian tradition[1] as well as the Weberian tradition.

But Parsons himself distinguishes between the Kantian and Weberian traditions. Whereas the Kantian problem is the matter of "empirical proof" of knowledge (Parsons 1967, 48), the Weberian

31

problem is the role of the scientist in constituting knowledge. The Kantian problem can be expressed by the question: "Is it empirically true?" (Parsons 1967, 149). This presupposes that validity depends on correspondence with empirical reality. By contrast, the Weberian problem can be expressed by the question: Under what conditions are facts regarded as scientifically valid? Parsons formulates:

> Here Weber's crucial concept is "value-relevance" (*Wertbeziehung*). Essentially what Weber said was that no matter how fully any given empirical propositions are validated, their inclusion in a body of knowledge about society is never completely independent of the value perspective from which those particular questions were asked [and] to which these propositions constitute answers. (Parsons 1967, 149)

These questions about knowledge may apply to the problem of order as well. To that extent, the Kantian question presupposes an absolute validity for empirical knowledge, and the Weberian problem is therefore rooted upon a "lower level of generality" (Parsons 1967, 149).

With reference to these two traditions, Parsons believes that we can grasp some kind of order in society, even though that understanding of order is doomed to be questioned and possibly changed. In this aspect, one can argue that Parsons exploits the Kantian problem and the Weberian problem *pari passu* to develop his theory of social order.

Following from the above, it should be clear that theory for Parsons is not a simple copy of reality. That is, theory should constitute far more than that,[2] including a "logical structure" (Parsons 1937, 7), and the logical structure of theory should show an order in the world. For Parsons, the empirical world is 'darkness,' it is chaotic, full of inconsistencies, discrepancies, and ambiguities, before it is examined theoretically.[3] Thus theory, for Parsons, attempts to do more than simply copy the real, empirical world; theory tries to generate "meaningful interpretations of its order" (Hamilton 1983, 69). Parsons suggests: "The structure of the conceptual scheme itself inevitably focuses interest on a limited range of such empirical facts. These may be thought of as a 'spot' in the vast encircling darkness, brightly illuminated as by a searchlight" (Parsons 1937, 16).

In other words, theory is a conceptual 'tool' (Bourricaud 1981, 37), or a 'filter' (Hamilton 1983, 64) for confirming the social order. Even after theory illuminates a part of the world, the rest remains hidden in darkness.

Because the purpose of theory for Parsons is to draw a desirable picture of the world (i.e., a picture of social order), theory must be "general" (1970) or "abstract" (1961, 32), based upon "analytical realism" (Parsons 1937, 730).[4] As Lemert points out, Parsons's analytical realism is "exceedingly bashful" in its relations with the empirical world (Lemert 1979, 100). Therefore, there is a fundamental gap between the empirical world and the world as it is represented in theory: For Parsons the real world appears uncertain, chaotic, and disorderly, but it can be "made orderly in theory" (Lechner 1991, 181).

Finally, we should note that Parsons wants to develop a theory of social order which is neither Utopian, like Locke's theory of the social contract, nor pessimistic, like Hobbes's theory of the social order as guaranteed only by a Leviathan. He sees these theories as extreme views of the relationship between the actor and his environment (Parsons 1937, 89–95).[5] Instead, Parsons chooses the middle ground.

Components of Social Order

In order to explore Parsons's understanding of social order and the modern world, I shall pay attention to some central concepts in Parsons's theory, such as value, norm, culture, function, pattern variable, integration, equilibrium, social system, internalization (or socialization), and the AGIL four-function paradigm (i.e., AGIL: Adaptation, Goal Attainment, Integration, and Latent Pattern-Maintenance). These are all closely related to the problem of order in Parsons' theory. Through careful readings of Parsons's original works, I will reveal the understanding of the world (i.e., social order) that Parsons arrives at with these concepts, and then examine this understanding to see how it might reflect some characteristics of modernity, as described in the previous chapter.

Values are central in Parsons's understanding of social order. Parsons believes, basically, that social order is possible on the basis of shared values, acquired through the process of internalization (Holton and Turner 1986, 9).

Parsons conceives of values as "patterns" (1969, 440–1). For Parsons, the value pattern (orientation) appropriate to a particular collectivity, role, or norm-complex is not "the general pattern of the system," but "an adjusted, specialized 'application' of it" (Parsons, 1966, 23). Parsons presents a picture of value patterns as adjustable, flexible, malleable, and inherently dependant upon the particular situation, rather than a reified picture of common values as fixed, changeless, and all-embracing. According to Parsons, value patterns are "always institutionalized in an interaction context" (1951, 38). Bourricaud points out in this regard that value patterns, as the criteria of our evaluations, are "not God-given"; they are neither "alien" nor "transcendent" (Bourricaud, 1981, 59). Put differently, because values are not objects or things but merely conceptions of the desirable, their existence depends upon human beings in particular circumstances. As Parsons notes:

There seem to be, in the literature of social science, two main approaches to the problem of conceptualization [of values]. One of these, which I reject, is what I like to call the "Chicago" approach, which I think originated in the work of Thomas and Znaniecki. This takes its departure from the dichotomy of "attitudes" and "values." In this formulation attitudes are properties or characteristics of *actors*, while values pertain to the *objects* to which the actors are oriented. The crucial difficulty with this concept lies in its identification of the distinction with the actor-object (or situation) dichotomy as *concretely* conceived . . . I should like to contrast this with a view that derives, I think, mainly on the one hand from Max Weber, and on the other from American anthropology, especially Clyde Kluckhohn. This is the view that a value is not a category of concrete object or a property of one but is, to use the anthropological word, a "pattern". . . . I therefore accept the first part of Kluckhohn's well-known definition of *values as conceptions of the desirable*. (Parsons 1969, 440–1)

Values . . . I understand to be *conceptions of the
desirable* . . . they [societal values] are conceptions of the
good type of society. When institutionalized, they are
such conceptions as are held by the members of the
society themselves. (Parsons 1967, 147)

And, for Parsons, the notion of value is inextricably or insepa-
rably related to the notion of choice (Bourricaud 1981, 59). Parsons writes: "An element of a shared symbolic system, which serves
as a criterion or standard for selection among the alternatives of
orientation which are intrinsically open in a situation may be called
a value" (1951, 12). In other words, even when they are institutionalized, shared values are not forced upon the individual. On
the contrary, values are selected by members within the process of
interaction.

With regard to the problem of choice, the concept of pattern
variables needs to be addressed.[6] For Parsons, interaction is conceived as involving a series of choices or selections of one or the
other of two possible alternatives of the pattern variables. Parsons,
in collaboration with Edward Shils, writes:

An actor in a situation is confronted by a series of major
dilemmas of orientation, a series of choices that the
actor must make before the situation has a determinate
meaning for him. The objects of the situation do not
interact with the cognizing and cathecting organism in
such a fashion as to determine automatically the meaning of the situation. Rather, the actor must make a series
of choices before the situation will have a determinate
meaning. Specifically, we maintain, the actor must make
five specific dichotomous choices before any situation
will have a determinate meaning. The five dichotomies
which formulate these choice alternatives are called the
pattern variables because any specific orientation (and
consequently any action) is characterized by a pattern of
the five choices. (Parsons and Shils 1951, 76)

We can now consider Parsons's understanding of values in
reference to the common criticisms that this has received. Much

of the conventional criticism of Parsons can be seen to follow from his claim that sociology is "the science which attempts to develop an analytical theory of social action systems in so far as these systems can be understood in terms of the property of common-value integration" (Parsons 1937, 76). This definition seems to have two implications: It seems to imply, first, that sociology should emphasize integration as the social function *par excellence.* Second, it seems to imply that common values are essential to the integration of society. Parsons's claim might even be understood as implying that society is nothing but a "system of values," or that every value system plays an important role in the integration of society (Bourricaud 1981, 40).

But Parsons never contends that common values are well or thoroughly institutionalized in every society, or that they completely integrate societies. Mark Gould argues that Parsons claims only that there will be "determinate consequences for societies when such values are absent" (Gould 1991, 96). In fact, Parsons states: "Of course it is clearly understood that 'integration' in this complete sense applies only to the abstract society; in this as in other respects it is a limiting case. Certainly neither Pareto nor the present author means to imply that concrete societies are in general even approximately perfectly integrated in this sense, or that their members are normally... conscious that there is any system of common ends" (1937, 247–8).

This suggests that Parsons does not argue that complete institutionalization always results in common values, nor does he argue that the presence of shared values guarantees social order. Rather, Parsons is saying that values are one of the various factors in the formulation of the social order, which raises "the probability that social order will be manifest" (Gould 1991, 96–7). In one of his earlier essays, Parsons notes: "It is advisable, though it should scarcely be necessary, to point out once more that we are merely arguing for the necessity of assuming that a common system of ultimate ends plays a significant part in social life. We are not arguing that the concrete reality may be understood completely, or even predominantly in such terms" (1991b, 242).

According to Parsons, values are ambiguous and indeterminate. The constraints imposed by values are not definite, and their effects are not predictable (Parsons 1969, 440; Bourricaud 1981,

155). "The paramount value system," as Parsons formulates, is relevant to the description of the "society as a whole," but it does not include norms, which differ between subsystems of society, or social groups (Parsons 1967, 8). In other words, contrary to the widespread critiques, Parsons is fully aware of the limitations of shared values.

Finally, Pattern variables may appear at first to be "*a priori* conditions" which are imposed on interaction. But the actor actually faces them as a matter of choice. Thus, one can say that for Parsons the actor is always "compelled to choose" (Bourricaud 1981, 62). In short, the pattern variables are intrinsically rooted upon interaction, which is characterized by a series of choices, and which takes place in a temporal process.[7] Many common criticisms of Parsons' theory of values and normative integration are therefore misguided, and belied by Parsons's writings.

Values are constituents of culture, because they are patterns at the cultural level (Parsons 1969, 441). Therefore, the discussion of values leads to the discussion of culture. What is culture (or the cultural system) in Parsons's theory? First, for Parsons, the cultural system is one of the "action systems," consisting of the individual actor, role (or, personality); the interactive system (or, society); and the system of cultural patterning (Parsons 1951, 27). What is most important is Parsons's objection to the tendency of reductionism, represented by three categories; culturalism, psychologism, and sociologism.[8] In other words, Parsons rejects determinism and reductionism.

Nevertheless, Parsons conceives of the cultural system (including values and symbols) as enduring.[9] Some critics have interpreted Parsons's claims about the temporal duration of the cultural system to mean that the cultural system causes or determines human behavior. But Parsons's theory is not culturally deterministic (or reductionistic), because culture is not conceived as something that could determine human behavior. Much of this is clear from the discussion of values above, but these comments can be expanded.

First of all, cultures are not eternal; cultures change and die. Next, culture is not compelling, "arbitrary," or a "closed totality" that confines all those who are "under its sway" (Bourricaud 1981, 296). In his work "On the Concept of Value–Commitments," Parsons remarks: "It is essential to think in terms of value systems;

complex action systems cannot be 'governed' by a single undifferentiated value, nor by discrete, unrelated, particular values conceived in terms of the 'culture traits' concept, as used by the 'historical' anthropologists" (Parsons 1969, 454).

Parsons even describes culture as "artifacts produced through the behavior" of members of society (Kroeber and Parsons 1958, 583), and as the product of systems of human social interaction (Parsons 1951, 15). Parsons's notion of culture leads us, perhaps surprisingly, to the fact that in the relationship between culture and individuals, the power proves to lie with the latter.

We can now introduce norms into the discussion. Norms have a "lower level of cultural generality than do values"[10] (Parsons 1967, 10). Norms, unlike values, "involve a reference to a situation" (Parsons 1967, 9). Moreover, norms are very seldom clear and explicit, even though they involve reference to a situation. According to Parsons, three further specifications should be included:

> The first specifies the categories of units to which the norm applies; this is the problem of jurisdiction. The second specifies what the consequences will be to the unit that conforms and to the unit that does not conform to the requirements of the norm (variations in degree are, of course, possible); this is the problem of sanctions or enforcement. Finally, the third specifies that the meaning of the norm shall be interpreted in the light of the character and the situations of the units to which it applies; this constitutes the problem of interpretation, which is roughly equivalent to the appellate function in law. (Parsons 1967, 9)

Therefore, for Parsons, the constraints imposed by the normative system on behavior in specific circumstances are not formidable, but limited.[11]

Thus, for Parsons, norms are not dictates or constraints. Rather, they offer only general guidelines, and are always open to question or reinterpretation. Certainly, Parsons does not suggest that normative systems strictly regulate or perfectly prescribe individuals' behaviors (Bourricaud 1981, 13). Similar to Bourricaud, Barry

Barnes argues that Parsons's understanding of norms is often ig-
nored by critics, and their tendency to conceive of norms as "causes
of action" is sometimes "intensified by the excessive 'determining
power' they attribute to [norms in Parsons's theory]" (Barnes
1995, 52).

Consequently, Parsons's view of internalization,[12] and its relationship to the problem of order are often misunderstood. For
Parsons, internalization does not describe the fact that the individual is thrown into a prison of common value. Rather, because
norms are not like laws of the physical world, they can only be
effective through internalization. Moreover, because of the ambiguity, vagueness, and ambivalence of norms, the successful internalization of norms cannot be guaranteed. In other words, Parsons's
notion of internalization does not exclude the possibility that
socialization will fail,[13] and does not exclude the possibility of
deviance (Parsons and Bales 1955, 178–86).

Thus, Parsons does not understand the normative system as
monolithic. Because of its limits and ambiguities, it is often thrown
into question. Deviance can not only raise questions about specific
rules, but also about the normative system *in toto*, because deviant
patterns can become legitimated (Parsons 1951, 292). In other
words, questions raised by deviance may "turn the tables on the
wider society" (Parsons 1951, 294), and the whole normative
system could be shaken from its roots to its summit.

If we understand Parsons's arguments that internalization always allows for deviance, we can also see that Parsons's picture of
society or social order includes the indeterminacy of norms vis-à-
vis human behaviors, the restructuring and redefinition of norms
by members of society, and finally the instability of society due to
the temporal nature of norms.

Parsons's notion of equilibrium is of interest here. Parsons's
principle of equilibrium is that "a system will tend to remain in a
given state" in other words, the *status quo*, "unless and until it is
disturbed by some influence from outside the system" (Parsons
1959, 631). But he does not think that a solid, perfect, and
everlasting equilibrium is possible. Parsons goes on to note that it
would be a "radically unrealistic assumption" to assume that most
empirical systems remain in solid equilibrium in "the optimum
consummatory state" (1959, 632).

According to Parsons, "states of the system (i.e., the relations between the unit of reference and other units) and states of the situation are continually changing" (1959, 632). One might put this more strongly by saying that there are only momentary or temporary *equilibria*, not a lasting *equilibrium*. Therefore, Parsons suggested that there are tremendous contradictions and discrepancies between actual states and ideal (unrealistic) states, for example, "the optimum consummatory state" (Parsons 1959, 632). The social system has the never–ending task of sustaining and constantly reconstructing an ad hoc, precarious equilibrium. More accurately, what seems like a stable system consists of a series of ceaselessly changing equilibria.

Parsons's theory of the four functions[14] never claims the existence of a fully integrated society. The interdependence of the four functions is not "automatically given," and Parsons suggests that the "maximization of all four, and probably of any two, is not possible in the same state of a given system" (Parsons 1959, 631). Parsons goes on to point out that "integration in this complete sense applies only to the abstract society" (1937, 247). Thus, as Holton and Turner argue, it is "wholly wrong" to regard Parsons's theory of the social system as "an analysis which is completely committed to the view of society as a stable, smoothly functioning, integrated whole" (1986a, 19). Therefore, it might be argued more broadly that uncertainty, unpredictability, irregularity, ambiguity, and instability remain in Parsons's general theory of action, even though it aims to show social order.

As a matter of fact, order is approached as problematical and precarious in Parsons' general theory. In his article "On Building Social Theory: A Personal History" (1977), Parsons himself notes that, "I have been widely accused by critics of being a last-ditch defender of order at any price, the ultimate price usually being interpreted to be fascism" (Parsons 1977, 70). But against this interpretation, he insists:

> I very much stand by the view that order in this sense is genuinely *problematical*, and that *the nature of its precariousness* and the conditions on which such order as has existed and may exist is not adequately presented in any of the views of human society which are popu-

larly current, regardless of political coloring. . . . Fortu-
nately the more perceptive of the critics have seen *order
as a problem, not as an imperative.* (Parsons 1977, 70;
emphasis added)

Given this understanding, we can ask how order (equilibrium,
integration) is even possible. As we have seen above, not even
values, norms, and culture, which are all known as crucial resources for social order, can directly or completely sustain order.
What else might contribute to social order? What about social
control? Parsons never claims that social control[15] is a key source
of maintaining social order. Rather, he suggests that social control
depends mainly and intrinsically on socialization (Parsons 1951,
297). Because there is no perfect socialization, as we have already
discussed, social control cannot play a key role in maintaining
social order.

What is the underpinning of social order? As discussed above,
Parsons does not conceive of social order as guaranteed, but rather
imperfect and problematic. Social order is also not a feature of society,
according to Parsons, but a result of theoretical investigation into the
social world. Thus, to the extent that Parsons sees order, it is neither
a complete order, nor a completely empirical order.

It is hardly a coincidence, then, that Parsons's understanding of social order recognizes or reflects many of the characteristics of modernity we explored in the previous chapter, especially
contingency, temporality, uncertainty, irregularity, instability, and
ambiguity.

AGENCY

It is sometimes remarked that Parsons's theory of action produces
the most dismal picture of determinism, or the most formidable
threat to any voluntaristic image of man, despite the fact that
Parsons himself names his theory of action the 'voluntaristic theory'
of action.[16] More specifically, most critics claim that in Parsons's
theory there is neither actor nor action; instead, there are only
roles and rehearsals.[17] Therefore, *Homo parsoniensis*[18] is seen as an
oversocialized being,[19] nothing more than a "cog" (Turner 1988,

73) in a huge social system of status roles. That is, the autonomy of human actors (agency) is said to disappear in Parsons's theory.

Recently developed sympathetic critiques of Parsons's theory, however, argue that those criticisms are misleading, because the autonomy of human actors (agency) is a vital aspect of Parsons's voluntarism as well as Parsons's social–cultural system.[20] For those in this camp, *Homo parsoniensis* is not a "cultural dupe" whose actions are determined by norms or the cultural system (Holton and Turner 1986b, 217), but a free individual. Norms and the cultural system do not threaten his freedom and subjectivity,[21] but rather allow, guarantee, or even promote them. To that extent, Parsons can be named an "individualist" (Bourricaud 1981, 100), or a proponent of "homocentrism" (Lemert 1978). In fact, Parsons himself wants to be received as an individualist, proclaiming that:

> I think I was able to remain completely true to Weber's famous "methodological individualism" with respect to which he maintained that action in a proper sense occurs only through the agency of individual human beings and that the "intentions" of these human beings, the meaning of their actions, and of their consequences to them "subjectively" are of the essence of the Weberian method. . . . To my knowledge I have never abandoned the perspectives which were thus worked out in *The Structure of Social Action.* (Parsons 1974, 56)

Nevertheless, I believe that neither the common critiques of Parsons nor the sympathetic interpretations of Parsons's theory are promising explanations of Parsons's voluntaristic theory of social action. In the former, unsympathetic critics who argue that Parsons neglects the autonomy of human actors (agency) turn out to reveal only their misunderstandings, or their unfamiliarity with Parsons's work, which defied such criticisms to the end. But in the latter case, sympathetic critics have failed to recognize how Parsons acknowledges the compatibility of human autonomy (agency) and social structure, and why this is so.

For example, in order to prove Parsons's voluntarism, Alexander argues that Parsons grants the individual actor free will (1983, 43;

1987a, 24), and that free will is for Parsons "an indispensable part of every theory" (Alexander 1987a, 24). Parsons himself, however, denies that the autonomy of human actors (agency) in his voluntaristic theory can be understood as free will. He writes: "Perhaps I may add a few comments of my own . . . the older philosophical views of the 'freedom of the will' never did constitute the primary basis of my own conception of the voluntarism which was an essential aspect of the theory of action" (Parsons 1974, 55). Considering Parsons's comments, Alexander's arguments cannot be a satisfactory account of Parsons's voluntarism, even though he wants to provide a sympathetic clarification of Parsons's position on human agency.[22]

It would be quite possible, I believe, to approach the problem of 'voluntarism' in Parsons's theory of action from another angle: modernity. Put differently, by relating his view of man to modernity, we can better understand Parsons's voluntarism, or institutionalized individualism. Of course, this approach is hardly new.[23] Nevertheless, many proponents of this approach seem to focus mainly on Parsons's explicit treatments of social change, including his studies on industrial societies, though these rarely deal with Parsons's theory of action, in other words, human agency and social order in his general theory. Like several other sympathetic critics of Parsons's work, they therefore fail to offer a satisfactory explanation of voluntarism, merely pointing out that Parsons emphasizes the autonomy of the human actor.

Concerning this problem, the approach I take is simple: if the world in Parsons's general theory reflects or shares similarities with some characteristics of modernity, it will not be surprising if his image of man does as well, because of the inextricable linkage of man and society. To continue this approach, Parsons's indebtedness to Georg Simmel must be discussed. Even though Parsons does not mention Simmel in *The Structure of Social Action* (1937), he definitely considers Simmel to be "most important" in the development of his theory.[24]

Although Parsons neither directly speaks of anonymity nor relates the concept of role to anonymity, Simmel's understanding of the inextricable relationship between anonymity and freedom could be helpful in understanding the image of man in Parsons's voluntarism, and could then be helpful in illustrating that the image of man in Parsons's theory has an affinity with that of modern man.

Needless to say, the world in Parsons's theory is a complicated series of social roles, which are impersonal social locations containing obligations to act in the proper ways. Such roles are anonymous, non-personal, and objective. Therefore, individuals in a complex of social roles are prone to be dealt with as anonymous and objective beings. As Harold Garfinkel remarks, Parsons's world can be characterized as a typified world.[25]

Most of Parsons's critics attack the typification of the world in his theory, sometimes lamenting the resulting loss of uniqueness of human behavior. However, Parsons always rejects such criticism, claiming *Homo parsoniensis* has autonomy. Nevertheless, the question of how this autonomy is possible is left unanswered by Parsons.

I believe that the concept of modernity could offer an important clue to understanding these issues. Yet, before exploring this, even simple phenomenological insights seem to be highly useful in explaining the autonomy of *Homo parsoniensis*, his freedom vis-à-vis roles. Natanson's insights are especially relevant here. Briefly speaking, typification shields us from the uniqueness of our existence, but it is certainly also true of typifications that they guarantee a sphere of freedom for us. As mentioned in the discussion of modernity above, typification and anonymity are bases of freedom. Therefore, the question of how it is possible for individuals to be autonomous in the typified world of Parsons's theory can be solved by this contribution from Natanson. Institutionalized individualism, which is offered as a reply to Wrong's arguments against the oversocialized concept of man, can therefore be understood as describing the autonomy of the individual within institutionalized anonymous roles. Again, it is plausible to claim that the autonomy Parsons sees is one allowed by the anonymity of roles.[26]

Parsons, however, neglects the other, darker, side of anonymity or typification.[27] Why does he do so? I believe it is because Parsons distinguishes the individual from the role, and looks primarily at the individual rather than the role.[28] Ironically, this perspective is often neglected by Parsons's critics, who accuse him of identifying the individual and the role. Parsons never identifies the individual with the role. He just speaks of "individual personalities in role" as one of the types of acting unit (Parsons 1967, 194). In Parsons's general theory, as Bourricaud aptly indicates, "there is no action without actor" (1981, 13). Like Bourricaud, Lemert also points out that Parsons would not be able to speak sociologically, "without man at the center" (1979, 107). In fact, Parsons's position on this matter is shown in several places. Some examples:

> ... The role is rather a sector in his behavioral system, and hence of his personality. For most purposes, therefore, it is not the individual ... that is a unit of social systems, but rather his role-participation. (Parsons 1961, 42)

> But since the typical individual participates in more than one collectivity, the relevant structural unit is not the "total" individual or personality, but the individual in a role. (Parsons 1967, 10)

> The unit of interpenetration between a personality and a social system is not the individual but a role or complex of roles. (Parsons 1977, 196)

Therefore, what is "programmed" (Parsons 1977, 172) is not the individual, but the role. *Homo parsoniensis* is not "boxed in" (Parsons 1982, 261),[29] and is not a "straw man" (Parsons 1962, 71). Rather, Parsons describes the actor as follows:

> ... each actor is both acting agent and object of orientation both to himself and to the others ... as acting agent, he orients to himself and to others, in all of the primary modes or aspects. The actor is knower and object of cognition, utilizer of instrumental means and himself a means, emotionally attached to others and an object of attachment, evaluator and object of evaluation, interpreter of symbols and himself a symbol. (Parsons 1977, 167)

Homo parsoniensis is not a "stooge" (Bourricaud 1981, 244), but a free man, whose "specific acts are not prescribed" (Parsons 1961, 41) by given goals, norms, or values. He or she is a chooser among many options.[30] He or she is also "responsive and flexible" (Bourricaud 1981, 101). And he or she is capable of learning, not in the sense of an individual confined by socialization, but in the sense of an individual with many possibilities.[31]

Earlier it was mentioned that the anonymity and typification of society *per se* allow and make available the autonomy of the individual. One can argue that Parsons's voluntarism is crucially related to the extensive anonymity of modernity. Although at first Parsons was not able to successfully explain how individual autonomy was possible, he later improved his theoretical account of human autonomy by reference to the increasing freedom within the market system. Parsons argues, for example, that the theme of the "generalized symbolic media of interchange"

> . . . plays a very central role with respect to the problems of freedom and voluntarism. It was, I think, rather firmly established by the classical economists that the establishment of a ramified market system enormously increased the range of freedom of participants in the market. . . . It has been our position that from a certain point of view the development of generalized media of interchange constitutes the highest level of institutionalization yet attained of opportunities for freedom of action of individual units in action system. (Parsons 1974, 56–7)

Parsons confesses that he wants to try to generalize this theme "beyond the social system itself to the level of general action" (Parsons 1974, 57).

It is plausible to suggest that Parsons considers roles to be symbolic media of exchange, just like money (Parsons 1977, 174). Parsons argues that generalized symbolic media only have "value in exchange" (Parsons 1977, 174), and this could be applied to roles. Put differently, roles, understood as generalized symbolic media, obtain their value only when in the process of exchange. A role, therefore, is a kind of token, for example, a symbolic token (Giddens), or a cliché (Zijderveld), in the fully anonymous, typified, and abstract world. In the midst of the unstable, uncertain, irregular, and unpredictable world, roles allow some degree of certainty, regularity, continuity, and tangibility, even though these remain temporal.[32]

We can therefore understand why Parsons wants both "freedom and predictability" (Barnes 1995, 53). Moreover, we can suggest a plausible explanation of how they are compatible. It can be argued that for Parsons the anonymity of roles is seen as fostering human agency, especially in modern society, rather than as a constraint or a cause of alienation.

Because modern man has multiple, anonymous roles, everything is unpredictable. To most ordinary people, that situation is burdensome. Only when one is acting in a specific role can he be relieved from the unpredictability of the moment. In unpredictable situations, using roles means avoiding time-consuming thought, for example, guessing, imagining, reasoning, or reflecting. Using roles therefore provides relief, and subsequently freedom. The unpredictable world becomes the predictable world for a moment. Predictability may increase freedom, by saving us from unnecessary thought.

We can see, therefore, that whereas Simmel explains both the autonomy and the alienation which result from anonymity, Parsons only addresses the former.[33]

But autonomy has another basis in Parsons's theory, as well. As discussed above, Parsons notes that social order (or society) is precarious or problematic, given the temporality, inconsistencies, and limitations of norms, values, and cultures. Thus, the individual is no longer bound. Norms, values, and culture come to be seen by individuals as vague and abstract, having nothing to do with them any more. Internalization, as a key institution for imposing society's ideal onto the individual, is no longer a formidable mechanism. The internalized norms are not homogenous, but heterogeneous.[34] Internalization is fated to be incomplete, because even at its most successful, the actor does not fully identify with the roles which society assigns by means of internalization. Because full socialization never occurs, it can be said that roles are something an actor has rather than is. And, Parsons goes on to point out: "Of course human behavior is not 'determined' by society as against the individual, nor is the obverse true" (Parsons 1962, 79).

Thus, society cannot determine the individual. It does not dissolve the individual in its "chemical bath" (Bourricaud 1981, 109), in an alchemical operation. Whereas society is characterized as an ambiguous entity, the individual in Parsons's general theory of action is depicted as an abstract being, an actor without qualities, simultaneously anonymous and free. The link between the individual and society seems weak, possibly broken.

What is important here is that autonomy vis-à-vis the role is shown to be a different type of autonomy than the type of autonomy which was discussed above, the type of autonomy allowed and fostered by role-taking. Autonomy vis-à-vis the role results from the separation (or distance) between the actor and the actor's roles. As Bourricaud aptly points out, Parsons places great emphasis on the distance that "in general separates an actor from his roles" (1981, 293).[35]

Parsons clearly thinks that the conception of agency in his general theory of action can be related to the autonomy of individuals in modern times, even though he makes no effort to develop this theme into a general theory of human nature.[36]

The above analysis suggests that Parsons's conceptions of human agency, as well as society (social order), reflect characteristics of modernity, especially the abstract nature of modern society, the mutual autonomization of the institutional order and the individual, the crisis of socialization, and more generally, freedom, anonymity, uncertainty, unpredictability, vagueness, instability, contingency, temporality, inconsistency, and ambiguity.

Parsons's Explicit Discussion of Modernity

So far we have examined the implicit image of modernity in Parsons's theory of social order and human agency. Before concluding, we will look briefly at Parsons's explicit observations of the modern world in his theory of social change. We will consider Parsons's conceptions of pluralism, role-pluralism, inclusion, adaptive upgrading, the vital center, value generalization, instrumental activism, institutionalized individualism, and diffusely enduring solidarity. With these concepts, Parsons provides us with a precise theoretical formulation addressing social order and the individual in modern society.

For Parsons, modern society is far less programmed, but offers more programs, than traditional society. That is, modern society is a "pluralistic" society (Parsons 1967, 429). Pluralism has "debunked" traditional values and ideas, which can no longer simply be taken for granted (Parsons 1969, 86, 91). Concomitantly, the individual is not "stably organized about a coherent system of values, goals, and expectations" (Parsons 1969, 84).

Pluralistic society provides the individual with "a considerable number of possible alternatives," not only with "one socially sanctioned definition of the situation" (Parsons 1969, 86). This includes roles, as well. Of course, as Parsons acknowledges, "role-pluralism is a central feature of all human societies" (1977, 170). The degree of role pluralism increases, however, "the more highly differentiated the society" (Parsons 1977, 170). Consequently, it is increasingly difficult for pluralistic society to bind the individual, and to tie the individual to his roles. A "fixed, one-to-one correspondence between the actor and his roles" becomes impossible.[37] The modern world therefore allows the individual emancipation, personal rights, and individual liberties (Parsons 1969, 87, 92), but at the same time causes a "state of insecurity" and "high levels of anxiety" (Parsons 1969, 84), an "enormous burden of decision" (Parsons 1969, 86), and a high incidence of anomie (1969, 86).

Despite the fact that modern society is full of "tensions" and "structural strains" (Parsons 1969, 92), it is prone to continuity (Parsons and White 1960). Parsons calls this tendency the "upgrading of adaptive capacity" (1977, 51). He also points to the process of "inclusion"[38] as a tendency in modern society, particularly American society. Inclusion is a tolerance of the unusual, and a stepping stone for the pursuit of homogeneity among heterogeneity. But the process of inclusion, in an uncertain and instable world, is based on a smaller and smaller common ground.

Inclusion is therefore inherently associated with "value-generalization" (Parsons 1977, 53). Value-generalization is easily translated into the levelling (or standardization) of value, or the abstraction of value. Put differently, a generalized value is an ambiguous and vague value. Because modern society is characterized by generalized values, there is also an "increasing looseness" between the individuals and the society (Parsons 1967, 429).

As illustrative examples of a "vital center" (Bourricaud 1981, 226) of value-generalization in contemporary American society, Parsons discusses "instrumental activism"[39] and "institutionalized individualism."[40] Such values are heavily rooted in Christianity. Behind these generalized values, society is conceived not as an "end itself," but rather as "the instrument of God's will" (Parsons 1964, 196). In secular terms, society "exists in order to 'facilitate' the achievement of the good life for individuals" (Parsons 1964, 196). To that extent, society has a "moral mission" (Parsons 1964, 196). However, the individual is also conceived not as an end itself, but as an instrumentality for the building the "Kingdom of God on Earth" (Parsons 1964, 196).

The 'functional diffusion' (Parsons 1977, 186) of these generalized values, or the 'vital center,' beyond the religious arena, has significant consequences. The originally religious instrumental activism has been transformed into a "worldly instrumental activism" in contemporary American society (Parsons 1991a, 52). Bourricaud formulates: "Just as God acts through the general will and issues impersonal commandments, society, too, lays down the rules of the game but leaves it up to each actor to play out his own hand. Nothing is rigidly spelled out in detail, and society has nothing to say about how the individual should go about his work, what he should do first and what last" (1981, 217).

Therefore, in Parsons's work, the term "institutionalized individualism" is used not only as a response to the charge of an "oversocialized image of man" on the level of his abstract, ahistorical general theory of action, but is also seen as a generalized value in contemporary American society.

Parsons does not indicate how solid the vital center of modern society might be. But his accounts of "ethnicity" in modern society (1977, 389) are suggestive. According to Parsons, "ethnically homogeneous entities" become rarer and rarer. Ethnic groups coexist as 'diffusely solidary collectivities' (Parsons 1977, 385–6). Ethnic identities and solidarities are 'empty symbols'—"empty of elaborate social distinctions," and are thus "able to function freely and smoothly in this multi-ethnic social system."[41] Ethnicity becomes a matter of "voluntary selectivity," not of fate (Parsons 1977, 391).

The process of inclusion requires, then, a higher-level concept than ethnicity, i.e., an all-embracing concept. This could perhaps be that of "nation" (Parsons 1977, 385) or "international order" (Parsons 1967).[42] These are characterized by a solidarity which is even more diffuse than the 'diffuse enduring solidarity' of ethnic groups (Parsons 1977, 385). It is, therefore, safe to conclude that the fragility of the 'vital center'—generalized values—is unprecedented in modernity. Put differently, the 'vital center' is too "vulnerable" (Holton and Turner 1986b, 231), and too abstract and vague to bind individuals to itself. Thus, the institutionalized individualism of modern society is reinforced, *a fortiori* (Parsons and Platt 1973, 447).

For modern men and women, the vital center appears tremendously abstract, intangible, indifferent, or even useless, like a distant relative. With even the idea of human dignity and freedom as feeble adumbrations, the remaining values are doomed to be deinstitutionalized, to use Gehlen's term. Therefore, the modern world Parsons sees is one in which no culture, norms, or values can ground the individual. The normative order of the modern world is hardly observable,[43] and only the 'factual order,' which is described by Parsons as a randomness, becomes remarkable and outstanding.[44] In other words, there can be no doubt that the empirical world Parsons witnesses is a fundamentally precarious, vulnerable, and fragile world. Thus, for Parsons, it is possible to speak of "the malaises and the moral evils" of contemporary society (Parson 1977, 58).

It should be noted, however, that Parsons never attempts to return to the *Gemeinschaft*. He defies to the end the intellectual "nostalgia for *Gemeinschaft*" (Parsons 1978, 152),[45] calling it the attempt of "de-differentiation" (Parsons 1977, 312). His view of modern society is optimistic, not pessimistic, in other words, he never adopts *fin-de-siecle* pessimism, because he observes that modern society allows an unprecedented autonomy, which outweighs the dark side of modernity.

To that extent, one can argue that Parsons is strikingly modern. That is, Parsons faces modernity and does not try to escape from it. The one temptation of nostalgia which Parsons might not resist is the "desire-for-the-whole." But even in this regard, Parsons wants a vague and abstract 'wholeness,'[46] which cannot undermine the autonomy of the individual. It allows autonomous individuals to get along with each other and live together. If one still wants to claim that it is a reification,[47] such a reification by no means undermines or attacks human autonomy or agency, because this 'wholeness' is abstract and vague.

In conclusion, it is not difficult to see Parsons's understanding of modernity, in his theory of the social order and the individual, as both analytical and empirical. Parsons sees the precariousness of the empirical world, so his understanding of the world in his general theory is not one of a very stable, solid world, even though his fundamental desire is to show the order of the social world.

3

ERVING GOFFMAN

The purpose of this chapter is to scrutinize the manner in which Goffman's work reflects an understanding of modernity.

There are diverse characterizations or interpretations of Goffman's work.[1] I do not propose to dwell here at length on surveying these characterizations.[2] It should be noted, however, that this variety of interpretations is partly due to the fact that Goffman never tried to form a "school" (Riggins 1990). But it also illustrates that sociologists are indebted to Goffman for a variety of reasons, whether they are sympathetic or critical. Most agree, moreover, that Goffman deals with some important aspects of modern societies, and even provides us with a profoundly astute analysis of modern world. Schudson even claims that Goffman is a "perfect analyst of modernity" (1984, 634).

To that extent, it is easier to see that Goffman's theory relates to modernity. But it should be noted that, although the modern world is an important subject to Goffman, he never sets out to construct a comprehensive theory of modernity.

Be this as it may, Goffman makes some highly astute observations about the modern world, and we find that there are two major appraisals of these observations: On the one hand, Goffman is seen as a Machiavellian cynic, on the other hand, he is seen as a moralist. The proponents of the former view argue that Goffman's

53

work characterizes individuals as amoral, pursuing their own selfish interests.[3] This appraisal is widespread in contemporary sociology. However, those who are in the latter camp claim that such criticisms are superficial and misleading. They argue, on the contrary, that his work is moral from its inception. Thus, they attempt to show how Goffman can be understood as addressing a number of commonly held values in our society.[4]

However, a third interpretation offers a somewhat different view. According to the third position, the first two interpretations both fail to appreciate his intention to identify and clarify the nature of social reality, including the problem of self and social order.[5] To understand Goffman's view of self and order, it is certainly necessary to go beyond the question of whether it is moral or not. Both of the first two views are plausible at a superficial level, but Goffman's work, upon closer reading, shows no rigid adherence to either view.

The position I will elaborate below begins with the third position. Thus, I shall deliberately try to detach Goffman's work from both major camps of critics. Creelan distinguishes three stages in Goffman's work. First, there is a naïve view of "ritual and moral rules" as the "structuring principles of social life" (Creelan 1984, 671–2). In this view, ritual and moral rules are conceived as sacred. Next, there is a period of cynical outrage over the fact that rituals and moral rules are "manipulated and exploited" by the haves or the "powerholders" in pursuit of their own self-interested goals (Creelan 1984, 672). Finally, Creelan argues, Goffman offers a "more complex, but ultimately hopeful understanding of sacred representation" (Creelan 1984, 671), especially, in his *Frame Analysis*—that is, according to Creelan, Goffman transcends his previous moral stage. Creelan goes on to argue that Goffman was never again so naïve as to confuse rituals with moral rules, or either with "the sacred symbol" with "its infinite references" (1984, 617).[6] Yet, Goffman never denies the possibility of the sacred impinging on human affairs.

I am concerned with neither the morality nor the amorality of Goffman's work, nor am I interested in outlining the stages of Goffman's work for historical purposes. What is of overriding concern is to look at Goffman's work on social order and self in the light of modernity. In other words, I wish to outline what aspects of Goffman's work on social order and agency reflect characteristics of modernity. I will therefore clarify certain aspects of his work that bear upon modernity. Throughout, I hope to eliminate misunderstandings of Goffman's work, and to take his original work seriously.

SOCIAL ORDER

In this section, I focus on Goffman's concepts of ritual, role, rule, norm, ritual order, ritual equilibrium, ritual disequilibrium, interaction order, frame, and framing process. I will elaborate upon the relationship between his views of order and modernity. I believe these views are best understood as having three stages in Goffman's career.

First, I will deal with the stage of Goffman's early writings, mainly his work from the 1950s.[7] As mentioned above, many theorists defend Goffman against the charge of amorality. Goffman's work is viewed as moral, especially his early work. For example, Creelan (1984) characterizes Goffman's early work as a naïve acceptance of ritual and moral rules as sacred, because Goffman seems to retain the tacit assumption that they are "the best for everyone in the society" (Creelan 1984, 672). Collins argues that Goffman is very close to Durkheim in seeing that "social reality is at its core a moral reality" (Collins 1988, 44). Collins points out that Goffman's emphasis on interaction ritual resembles Durkheim's focus on religious ritual; both are mechanisms by which "moral sentiments are produced and shaped into specific social forms" (Collins 1988, 44).

However, we need to be skeptical of these perspectives, even though Goffman does confer somewhat of a sacred value upon ritual as holding manifold moral possibilities. These perspectives imply that Goffman equates social reality (or society), ritual, moral rules, and the sacred. But is Goffman convinced that ritual, society, or the world are the locations of the sacred and moral? Does he really deem that ritual is used only as a means or mechanism for the allegedly sacred and moral society?

We need to consider Goffman's work with reference to modernity. Goffman never naively equated society and ritual with the moral and sacred, nor did he conceive of ritual as a necessary factor or condition for constituting the sacred and moral society. In other words, from the beginning, the world Goffman witnesses is not at all a world which is fundamentally moral and sacred. Rather, it is impossible for Goffman to observe that kind of world. The splendid facets of the world that Goffman sees in his early period make society appear as if it is sacred and moral *in nucleo*, but moral rules and norms have been severely undermined. The world Goffman examines is one in which everything is thrown into question, shaken and destroyed, ranging from moral rules, norms, and sacred values, to the Sacred *per se*. The world in Goffman's work, particularly in his early period, clearly shows aspects of modernity, elaborated above.

Let us look at the manner in which Goffman's early writings reflect the modern world we have depicted above. First of all, he observes that the traditional institutional order is no longer taken for granted, and has faded away, or at best, remains in a state of ambiguity. Thus, it is hard to observe traditional order or society. Under these circumstances, the rules and norms of society appear no longer binding for individuals. In his article, "The Nature of Deference and Demeanor" (1967), Goffman writes: "The rules of conduct which bind the actor and the recipient together are the bindings of society. But many of the acts which are guided by these rules occur infrequently or take a long time for their consummation. Opportunities to affirm the moral order and the society could therefore be rare" ([1956] 1967, 90).

In such a world, which can no longer bind individuals, behavior is unpredictable, unstable, and uncertain. In the midst of uncertainty, the behaviors of everyday life can be viewed as an unpredictable "wild card" (Manning 1992, 34), or a continuous game of "concealment and search" (Goffman 1953, 84).

Under such circumstances, characterized by a high degree of uncertainty and ambiguity, Goffman seeks something to provide some degree of certainty, clarity, and stability for individuals. For Goffman, it is "ceremonial rules" which fulfill this function (1967, 53).[8] Ceremonial rules are seen not only as substituting for the institutional order, including "law, morality, and ethics" (Goffman 1967, 55), but are also considered as a kind of orderliness or order, which can bind individuals and provide them with a "guide for action" (Goffman 1967, 48). Moreover, Goffman goes on to argue that there is a slightly different dimension of order, which is likely to arise from or accompany the same scenes in which ceremonial rules are enacted or prevail. Goffman names it "ritual order" (1967, 44). It is order arranged at the moment, and becomes perceived as orderliness embodied by the participants' interaction using (or in accordance with) ceremonial rules or rituals. In other words, while the traditional order is crashing down, Goffman's search for order leads to the ritual order.

How and why does Goffman pay so much attention to ritual as a remarkable order in modern times? There is a clue in Goffman's article, "On Cooling the Mark Out" (1952). In this paper, Goffman deals with victims and their difficulties adapting to loss in criminal fraud cases. He refers to three main characters in the situation: the con, the mark (the victim), and the cooler. The cooler is a curious character, whose role needs to be explained. The cooler is an accomplice of the con, and has "the job of handling persons who have been out on a limb," in other words, the mark (1952, 452). This job is called "cooling the mark out" (1952, 452). After the fraud occurs the cooler attempts to give the mark "instruction in the philosophy of taking a loss" by exercising "the art of consolation" (1952, 452).

What is important here is that Goffman does not restrict his attention simply to criminal fraud cases. Goffman wants to expand the implications to "an understanding of some relations in our society" (1952, 451). Thus, Goffman argues that "cooling the mark out is one theme in a very basic social theory" (1952, 453). Goffman is bent on showing that the modern world is a place in which chaos, such as that seen in criminal fraud cases, occurs frequently. He thus compares the modern individual to the mark, who is in trouble and cannot handle the situation by himself.

What are the sources of chaos in modern society? First of all, chaos results from the collapse of the world taken for granted and the loss of the ability to predict behavior by means of usual patterns. Second, an unbearable chaos results when a situation contains tremendous discrepancies or contradictions. Although Goffman never uses the term 'pluralism,' these sources of chaos may remind us of pluralism (discussed above in regards to modernity). Everything becomes shaken and topsy-turvy due to pluralism as well. We have already looked at individuals in pluralistic situations, and we know they experience bewilderment.

Within a similar context, Goffman suggests that if the mark's 'blow-up' is "too drastic or prolonged, difficulties may arise" (1952, 458). Under chaotic circumstances, the individual, like the mark, becomes "disturbed mentally" or "personally disorganized" (1952, 458). It is hard for either to figure out "what's going on?" According to Goffman, in order to maintain the situation and keep going, the disturbed individual "must be carefully cooled out" (1952, 456). Thus, individuals, like the mark, need some way to figure out the ongoing situation, to help them 'cool out,' in other words, to define and adjust to the situation. At the moment, as Goffman points out, the role of the cooler is to serve as a pain-killer, to "pacify and reorient" the disturbed individual (1952, 461). Thus, the cooler sends him back to "an old world or a new one," so that he can "no longer cause trouble to others or can no longer make a fuss" (1952, 461). Therefore, the cooler is seen as offering a kind of relief and "comfort" (1952, 461). As Goffman points out, the occupation most responsible for 'cooling' individuals is that of psychotherapy (1952, 461).

But, beyond these examples of specific roles, Goffman considers the role itself as one of the most significant conduits for giving the individual comfort. Goffman points out the possibility that the disturbed individual can "seek comfort" in his social roles (1952, 461). To that extent, the role is serving the same function as the cliché, which Zijderveld explores. And both the role and the cliché can be seen as tokens, which not only provide individuals with some degree of clarity, predictability, and stability, but also allow them to connect with each other smoothly.

The description above is merely one illustration of the precariousness of the ritual order and efforts to maintain the ritual order in the face of this precariousness. This dynamic of the ritual order is suggested by the concept of "ritual equilibrium"[9] (Goffman 1967, 45). It can be said without exaggeration that, for Goffman, the ritual order is based primarily upon a momentary equilibrium that is sustained in a tenuous balance by the members in social interaction. Its certainty is inherently temporary, and therefore, its comfort is also essentially superficial, fragile, ephemeral, and even deceitful by nature. Finally, Goffman suggests, the comfort the individual gets from the ritual order is nothing but bamboozling or "stalling" (1952, 458).

Goffman's understanding of order, therefore, has nothing to do with the sacred, or with morality, in any traditional sense. The individual cannot expect real comfort, or lasting relief, because the fragility of order results from its very temporality and contingency. At best, the individual can experience a limited relief in the repetitiveness which makes reflection unnecessary. In other words, the ritual order described by Goffman allows the modern individual pseudo-certainty. If one understands this, it is not surprising that Goffman sees ritual interaction not as a scene of harmony, but as an "arrangement for pursuing a cold war" (1953, 40), and not surprising that he claims, "the main principle of the ritual order is not justice but face" (1967, 44). Ritual equilibrium must be understood as a subtle balance which can be disrupted, leading to 'ritual disequilibrium' (Goffman 1967, 19).

Thus, even though the ritual order, as a functional substitute for the traditional-institutional order, provides some degree of certainty and clarity in modern times, it is basically unstable and hypocritical, in Goffman's understanding.[10]

Before turning to Goffman's next stage, we might mention Goffman's discussion of the possibility that severely disturbed individuals might adhere to their roles in order to seek comfort and avoid instability and uncertainty. In other words, he suggested that individuals could, like drug addicts or alcoholics, become obsessed with a role, pour themselves into "one role," and identify themselves with it, believing that the predictability and regularity of a role could cure their "injuries" (1952, 461). Goffman warned, however, that it is very difficult for the individual to escape from burdens by means of a role, and such attempts are doomed to fail, and could even "destroy him" (1952: 461).

The reasons for this are easily stated. First, it is impossible in modern life for an individual to live in only one role. There are many roles, diverse and contradictory, before and around the individual (1952, 456). They require a continuous redefinition of self. Second, in modern society, there is a tendency to believe that identification with a role is a "false claim" (1952, 461). Perhaps even those who try to escape into roles are aware that there is really no essential connection between themselves and their roles.

I shall return to this important issue below, but it is essential to point out here that Goffman is conscious of the inherent discrepancy between the self and its roles. Moreover, Goffman suggests that the role cannot completely overwhelm the individual, but, rather, the individual manipulates the role, and is never faithful to it.

Let us turn to Goffman's next period. In this phase, what were once glimmering suspicions about the ritual order come to the fore. The precariousness of ritual equilibrium, namely, "ritual disequilibrium" (Goffman 1967, 19, 24), and "ritual vulnerability" (Goffman 1983b, 4), become core themes in this stage. To put it simply, Goffman's work in this period[11] further disproves that he was naïve concerning the ritual order. Whereas in his early work the ritual order was viewed as a sort of painkiller, in his second period, it is a painkiller which doesn't work, but rather profits a conspiracy of doctors, pharmacists, and drug companies.

The understanding of the ritual order evident in the second period is based on the realization that ambiguity and uncertainty characterize even the new-found ritual order. In other words, the predictability and stability provided by the ritual order is temporary and inherently fragile *in nucleo*. We therefore arrive at a dismal picture of the world; it is even more ambiguous, opaque, and uncertain than before. It is finally viewed as a sordid game of hanky-panky (Goffman 1961a; 1961b; 1963a; 1963b; 1967; 1970; 1971; 1981a; 1983a; 1983b) or a theatrical drama (Goffman 1959). Thus, for Goffman, order is undermined again with the realization that the ritual order, as well as the institutional order, is ambiguous and uncertain. Individuals therefore suffer a double impact.

The situation is even worse, because the vagueness and ambiguity of the ritual order allow it to be easily distorted and manipulated by individuals for selfish purposes. The picture of the individual taking advantage of the ambiguity of the ritual order is expressed well by the term "working the system" (Goffman 1961a, 210), if we extend this, *mutatis mutandis*, beyond the case of inmates and staff in asylums. Goffman's image of man now resembles a Machiavellian swindler. Goffman now describes the world cynically, as a place in which "reality" might be "considerably twisted" (1961a, 384).

Not to put too fine a point to it, Goffman attempts to capture the other face of the world, in other words, the squalid side of the world, which comes to be seen as a field of conspiracy,[12] full of all kinds of tricks and machinations. Rules and norms are no longer significant elements of the institutional order.[13] Furthermore, "the ceremonial rule" (Goffman 1967, 54) and the "ritual norm,"[14] which have taken the place of traditional rules and norms in providing "guides for action" (Goffman 1967, 48; 1971, 95), are also ambiguous. Goffman, indeed, argues that most of these new rules and norms are "little explicated," "leave many matters tacit," and are "almost always couched in general forms," so they are intrinsically vague (1971, 97). Consequently, they are prone to be exploited by individuals for their own egoistic ends.

Goffman deliberately makes an effort to reveal that widespread social notions, highly abstract and vague, no longer directly affect the conduct of people, and at best, remain values in name only. Values and the ritual order can be used, exploited and manipulated by individuals in defensive, self-justifying, and egoistic ways.[15] Goffman goes on to describe public life in modern times as a "battlefield" (1971, 328). Just as the life of animals can be seen as oscillating between tranquility and mobilization (1971, 328), the life of human beings in modern public places can be viewed as a cutthroat combat zone, in which people seemingly "go about their business," but, at the same time, "get ready to attack or to stalk or to flee" (1971, 238). For Goffman, the sense of "peace" or "security" (1971, 328–29) is nothing but a disguised calm in the face of insecurity, like the eye of a storm. In his *Relations in Public* (1971), Goffman formulates that ". . . we might better ask of the most peaceful and secure [situation] what steps would be necessary to transform it into something that was deeply unsettling. And we cannot read from the depth of the security the number of steps required to reverse the situation" (1971, 329). Here, Goffman reveals that the banal solace offered by the ritual order, as well as that affected by the institutional order, is not a real consolation.

What is more distressing than the "vulnerability of public life" in modern society (Goffman 1971, 331), however, is that we ourselves are actually making the world, in other words, the world is an outcome of a "working consensus" (Goffman 1959, 10, 65), which is characterized as a *"modus vivendi"* (Goffman 1959, 9). This is proven by the fact that even in a total institution[16] such as a mental hospital, military camp, or jail (which are as compelling, heavy-handed, and oppressive as human institutions can be), it is the "persistent conscious effort" of members, who are trying to "stay out of trouble," that creates and maintains the reality within it (Goffman 1961a, 43).[17]

"Normal appearance" (Goffman 1971, 238), as it is called, is constructed and sustained through the working consensus *ad interim*, until this delicate working consensus is disrupted. Put differently, normal appearance is precarious,[18] uncertain, unstable, and ambiguous, and is easily transformed into a dangerous situation. Goffman states: "Social arrangements for the most part are inherently ambiguous, meaning here that the interactional facts are only loosely geared to structural ones" (1971, 224). And: "Behind these normal appearances individuals can come to be at the ready, poised to flee or to fight back if necessary. And in the place of unconcern there can be alarm—until, that is, the streets are refined as naturally precarious places, and a high level of risk becomes routine" (1971, 332). Moreover, for maintaining normal appearances, the art of performance, the "art of impression management" (1959, 208), is *de rigueur*. In this connection, our everyday life is seen as a series of "strict tests" of our ability to maintain normal appearances, which we "must pass" (Goffman 1959, 55).

In short, Goffman focuses on the ritual order during a time when the institutional order has vanished. As soon as Goffman sees some sort of regularity and stability in the ritual order, however, he realizes that the ritual order is much more easily manipulated by individuals because of its inherent vagueness and instability. Concomitantly, the entire world of everyday life is viewed as plunging into ambiguity and uncertainty. Goffman expresses this situation in terms of the concepts of ritual equilibrium, the precariousness of ritual equilibrium, and ritual disequilibrium. Moreover, Goffman looks into the physical environment of social interactions to vividly show the danger and fragility resulting from the opaqueness and uncertainty of the modern world.

To continue with the analysis, it should be pointed out that Goffman discovers and focuses on another dimension of order, the order emerging from efforts and adjustments to "avoid collision" (1971, 6).[19] To use the analogy of driving, there is an order that results from continuously monitoring, adjusting and coordinating[20] with other cars[21] on the road.[22] Goffman calls this type of order the "interaction order" (1983b). After scrutinizing the ritual order and its precariousness, it is this order which Goffman turns to and identifies as a most significant order in modern society.

Specifically, the interaction order is located in the "domain of activity" (Goffman 1983b, 5). In other words, it is an "order of activity" (Goffman 1983b, 5). Whereas in premodern society 'social order' referred to an entirely different order, in modern society the institutional order has lost influence on individuals, and it is the interaction order that remains. The interaction order becomes remarkable as the only significant order for explicating the arrangement of activity. Its tenacious endurance might be seen as reflecting an ahistorical feature of human relationships.

What, then, is the nature of the interaction order? How does the interaction order continue to order human life? Furthermore, why does it appear to be necessitated by "certain universal preconditions of social life" (Goffman 1983b, 3). For Goffman, the interaction order should be considered as an order in its own terms. It seems to have nothing to do with the institutional order in the sense of a causal relationship. Goffman also states that "No implications are intended concerning how 'orderly' such activity ordinarily is, or the role of norms and rules in supporting such orderliness as does obtain" (1983b, 5), even though, conventionally viewed, the "workings of the interaction order" are "the consequences of systems of enabling conventions," in other words, the institutional order, and appear to be based upon a "social contract" and "social normative consensus" (1983b, 5). Goffman argues it would be foolish to see the workings of the interaction order as they are viewed commonsensically. This is not only because the presumed motives for "adhering to a set of arrangements need tell us nothing about the effect of doing so," but there is also a "large base of shared cognitive presuppositions" for the orderliness (1983b, 5). Individuals "go along with current interaction arrangements for a wide variety of reasons" (1983b: 5).

In Goffman's analysis, the interaction order and the institutional order have become increasingly disconnected, a situation sometimes referred to as "loose coupling" (Goffman 1983b, 11). This loose coupling is accelerated by the abstraction of modern society, *a fortiori*. Due to the vicissitudes of the institutional order[23] and due to the loose coupling between the institutional and the interactional orders, the interaction order becomes the most prominent, important, living, enduring order. Goffman comments, for example:

> In general, then, (and qualifications apart) what one finds, in modern societies at least, is a nonexclusive linkage—a "loose coupling"—between interactional practices and social structures, a collapsing of strata and structures into broader categories, the categories themselves not corresponding one-to-one to anything in the structural world, a gearing as it were of various structures into interactional cogs. Or, if you will, a set of transformation rules, or a membrane selecting how various externally relevant social distinctions will be managed within the interaction. (1983b, 11)

Based upon the understandings of the basic nature of the interaction order, Goffman focuses on the increasing development of 'service transactions' in modern society (1983b, 14). Service transactions, partly because they are highly anonymous, carry the following basic understanding: "all candidates for service will be treated 'the same' or 'equally,' none being favored or disfavored over the others" (1983b, 14). Goffman discusses a "queuing arrangement" as a representative example. In queues, there is only a "temporal ordering" in accordance with the vague rule, "first come first served" (1983b, 14); all "externally relevant attributes," which are seemingly "of massive significance outside the situation," such as roles and statuses, are "held in abeyance" (1983b, 14–5).[24]

How stable is the interaction order, in Goffman's eyes? For Goffman, the interaction order, especially in modern society, is inherently fragile, because its basic principles, such as "equality" and "courtesy" in service transactions, are enacted in an ad hoc manner, differing case by case. Goffman observes: "But obviously, what in fact goes on while the client sustains this sense of normal treatment is a complex and precarious matter" (1983b, 15). Moreover, Goffman goes on to argue that notions of "equality" or "fair treatment" are themselves even more ambiguous concepts.

In other words, there is no objective algorithm for treating people equally or fairly. Thus, Goffman formulates:

> One can hardly say that some sort of objectively based equal treatment ever occurs, except perhaps where the server is eliminated and a dispensing machine is employed instead. One can only say that participants' settled sense of equal treatment is not disturbed by what occurs, and that of course is quite another matter. A sense that "local determinism" prevails doesn't tell us very much as to what, "objectively" speaking, does in fact obtain. (1983b, 16)

Goffman indicates the intrinsically fragile nature of the interaction order, in which the principles underlying the specific situation are generally if not necessarily ambiguous. In Goffman's eyes, there is ultimately no hope of order in modern society, in the sense of providing the individual with clarity and certainty.

Finally, we come to Goffman's last stage. Whereas in his earlier work he emphasized the dangerous and fragile nature of the social environment and the interactions within it, in Goffman's longest and most ambitious book, *Frame Analysis* (1974), he focuses on the cognitive dimension of the situation. In doing this, Goffman necessarily touches on the problem of the domain of the real, that is, he typically asks question about matters of reality. To pursue this, Goffman introduces the concept of "frames" or "frameworks" (1974, 10).[25] It should be clear, however, that these refer to "the structure of experience which individuals have at any moment of their social lives,"[26] not to "the structure of social life" (1974, 11, 13). Specifically, frames are viewed as a sort of conceptual tool or device, which the individuals use for figuring out the "purely cognitive sense of what it is that is going on" (1974, 439). If a frame is utilized successfully in a particular situation, cognitive stability would be sustained temporarily.[27]

Let me explain the nature of frames and Goffman's intentions. Individuals are encompassed with unprecedented pandemonium in modern society. Yet, even under these conditions, they are not completely abandoned in a sea of chaos, having no help. Just like a beacon, frames provide individuals with perspectives or interpretations about the particular situation. At this moment, one might recollect the function of roles and rituals (ceremonial rules and ritual norms) which Goffman introduced in his previous periods. Frames play the same role, but in cognitive aspects. In fact, Goffman points out that a "framework allows its user to locate, perceive, identify, and label a seemingly infinite number of concrete occurrences defined in its terms" (1974, 21). In this point, Goffman tries to identify the nature of frames. However, it should be emphasized that Goffman's overriding concern is with showing the precariousness and "vulnerability of frameworks" (1974, 10, 439), as he explores the precariousness of the ritual order and the interaction order. In other words, throughout the analysis of frameworks, Goffman wants to address the cognition of individuals facing increasing ambiguity and uncertainty.

Goffman approaches the vulnerability and fragility of frames in two ways: by noting their intrinsic changeability, and noting the human being's tenacious tendency to transcend frames. First of all, even though the frame is an inter-subjective "concept" (1974, 25), which "produces a way of describing the event to which it is applied" (1974, 24), it can easily be changed and transformed. Goffman explains the fragility of frames by means of the concept of 'keying' (1974, 44).[28] Moreover, during any one moment of activity "several frameworks" are likely to be applied by an individual or among individuals (1974, 25). Therefore, the individual can be "wrong in his interpretations, that is, misguided, out of touch, inappropriate, and so forth" (1974, 26). Furthermore, frameworks can be intentionally and meticulously designed, that is, they can be fabricated.[29] In modern society, due to the plurality of frameworks, each of which can be transformed, individuals can become bewildered and confused within the "multiple laminations of experiences" (1974, 182). Moreover, one might think that our world is nothing but a "deception or an illusion" (1974, 111). This undermines belief in all types of frames, and they can be experienced as fabrications, as opposed to being reified.

The second source of vulnerability in frameworks arises from the human capacity for transcendence. In regard to this, Goffman focuses on the "out-of-frame activity" of human beings (1974, 201). According to Goffman, individuals are prone to "pursue a line of activity—across a range of events that are treated as out of frame" (1974, 201), which is viewed as a unique "capacity" of human beings (1974, 201). The out-of-frame activity is carried out by subordinating, or dissociating from, the perspective of the particular ongoing situation itself (1974: 202). In other words, the individual is always ready to escape or elude the main activity in the particular situation, even while he seems to be deeply involved with the situation. For instance, while one is driving his car on the highway, he can look at a highway advertising, listen to the radio, or fantasize (1974, 215, 561). This illustrates that "a main line of activity can be carried on simultaneously with channels of out-of-frame doings" (1974, 237).

It is important to note that there are devices used to maintain the individual's orientation to a certain framework. Goffman calls this holding process the "anchoring of activity" (1974, 247). Among the devices used to anchor activity, Goffman mentions the supply of "routine services" (1974, 250). For instance, in order to gamble for long periods, gamblers need drinks, snacks, and a bathroom. Individuals are comforted by such services, and can remain within a particular framework of activity longer than they originally planned; Goffman observes, "all this routine servicing allows individuals to take the matter for granted and to forget about the conditions that are being quite satisfied" (1974, 250).

What is even more important for us here is the term "routine," which Goffman speaks of in regard to these services. Such services have to be familiar, for example, from other frameworks; that is, familiar things are likely to give some sort of relief, to allow the individual to keep going in, or stay longer at, the particular framework.

It should be noted, however, that Goffman considers the anchoring of activity as a deception or illusion, in other words, a kind of bad faith, and for several reasons. First of all, such anchoring leads the individual to forget the possibility of other frameworks, and dwell in one framework of activity without questioning or doubting the frame. Second, in the process of anchoring, the individual is likely to confuse the attraction of the framework itself with the attraction of routine services associated with it. Most of the time, individuals are baited by routine services, rather than attracted to a particular framework itself.

Goffman lists the five major devices or ways of anchoring activity in modern society: "Episoding Conventions," "Appearance Formulas," "Resource Continuity," "Unconnectedness" and "Human Being" (1974, 251–300). "Episoding conventions" "mark off" a particular framework from the "ongoing flow of surrounding events" (1974, 251). An example of an "appearance formula" is providing a role to an individual in order to anchor him into a particular framework (1974, 269). "Resource continuity" refers to the relative endurance of resources, allowing the individual certainty, and relief from reflection. Examples are "style" and a taken-for-granted "manner of doing things" (1974, 290). "Unconnectedness" refers to the tendency of regarding one framework's activity as having no connection with another framework's activity (1974, 292). Without the concept of "human being," in the sense of a perduring [enduring] self, Goffman indicates, it is impossible to "talk about the anchoring of doings in the world," because the self as "human being" is viewed as a ground for individuals to connect with each other in the world (1974, 293).

In Goffman's view, there are different types of bait, entertainment or amenities that seduce individuals into a particular framework and hold them on longer. These could include not only drinks in a casino, but a lovely wife, status, power, or money. However, even though modern society is equipped with various breathtaking anchoring devices and routine services, the anchoring of activity becomes disturbed, mainly by the unimaginable variety of anchoring devices in modern society.[30] Certainly, pluralism threatens the anchoring of activity. In other words, a number of options make it difficult for the individual to maintain attention to only one thing.

A large portion of Goffman's *Frame Analysis* is devoted to describing what happens when the process of anchoring is made difficult. He depicts two possibilities: troubles and the breaking of frames. Disturbances of anchoring bring about "ordinary troubles" (1974, 301), because it is very difficult for the individual to figure out 'what's going on here?' In other words, the individual is confused, bewildered, and thrown into doubt due to "ambiguity" and "uncertainty" (1974, 305). And, when such ambiguity and uncertainty are "wrongly resolved" (1974, 308), it leads to "errors of misframing" (1974, 316), such as "misperception" (1974,

308) and "miskeying" (1974, 311). Thus, "frame disputes" (1974, 324) will also be possible.[31] Under these circumstances, most people try to "clear the frame" (1974, 338), because they experience the unclear situation as a burden. It is a distressing fact that in reality, especially in modern times, it is a difficult feat to clear a frame. This is because, in reality, there is no clear-cut resolution, like "Smile, you're on Candid Camera" (1974, 339). Therefore, most unclear situations remain ambiguous.

Beyond the level of ordinary trouble, there is a more severe possibility, of "breaking frame" (1974, 345), which means breaking "the applicability of the frame," or "a break in its governance" (1974, 347). Goffman distinguishes two ways of breaking frame: explicitly and implicitly.

There are two varieties of explicit frame breaking, 'flooding in' (1974, 358) and 'flooding out' (1974, 350). 'Flooding-in' refers to the situation of an individual who is first outside a framed activity, such as an "uninvolved bystander," and then becomes involved. There is also the central possibility of 'flooding out,' breaking out of a particular framework, for example, "dissolving into laughter or tears or anger, or running from an event in panic and terror" (1974, 350).[32]

Besides the explicit possibilities of 'breaking frame' in terms of flooding-out and flooding-in, there are also possibilities for implicitly 'breaking frame': "downkeying" (1974, 359) and "upkeying" (1974, 366). Downkeying refers to the process of 'acquiring reality' (1974, 363), as when "mock acts become real ones" (1974, 359). In contrast, 'upkeying' refers to the process of losing reality. In other words, it refers to "a shift from a given distance from literal reality to a greater distance, an unauthorized increase in lamination of the frame" (1974, 366), for example, a shifting "from practice to 'as-if' games" (1974, 366).

The above four possibilities are all viewed as ways of undermining an initial frame of activity. They can all decrease or increase the individual's "distance from the initial activity, thereby adding or subtracting a lamination from the frame of his response" (1974, 359).

Goffman does not mention this, but the possibilities for upkeying and downkeying might be increasing in modernity, and it might be easier to upkey or downkey as well. Modern man capriciously downkeys and upkeys from frameworks. In other words, as soon as he is too deeply enthralled by a particular framework, he might try to escape.[33] For example, lovers who fall in love easily and rapidly can split apart rapidly as well.[34] Or a student can be engrossed in writing a dissertation, with a kind of ineffable jubilation, and the next moment become sick and tired and discouraged, and leave his desk. Perhaps all this coming and going, this upkeying and downkeying, arises mainly from the fact that the framework is chosen by us rather than given to us. One can say that the possibility of frame breaking is more likely in modern society than pre-modern society, because modern society is seen as a world of choice.

As is suggested above, in *Frame Analysis* Goffman tries to describe "the precariousness of the frame"—no more, but also no less (1974, 354). Thus, Goffman devotes considerable space to an exploration of the vulnerability of frames. One can, therefore, raise the question of why Goffman attempts to expound upon the precariousness of the frame? First of all, in his final analysis of the frame, Goffman wants to show the ultimate fragility of social life itself. The upshot of this is quite simple. Behind the fragility of the organization of experience (frameworks), Goffman arrives at the weaknesses of the framing process (1974, 439). And, finally, Goffman points out "weak points in social life" (1974, 463).[35] It is ultimately the finitude, mortality, and hollowness of frames and social reality that Goffman wants to show through frame analysis.

With that in mind, Goffman would like to raise a somewhat deeper issue, that of "other possibilities" (1974, 489). In the deepest layer of Goffman's work there is a quest for a solid, perfect certainty, the Sacred, and the Truth, beyond the imperfect frameworks of social life. In other words, the vulnerability of frameworks prompts Goffman to suggest that our attentions turn toward other possibilities, which are never fragile, imperfect, or deceitful, but firm, perfect, and truthful, possessing none of the weakness of being. Of course, for Goffman, questions of this kind, especially questions of the ultimate Other Possibility (or Being), are undoubtedly implicit, although his suggestions of other possibilities appear elsewhere in his *Frame Analysis*. For example, Goffman examines laughter and jokes as another way of accessing "other possibilities," when the laughter or joke applies to serious matters. Here we might just quote an example of a person who is forced to face death by the occasion of discussing his will: "The ceremony surrounding the execution of the will tries to be noble and solemn. In the office of a large law firm, the ceremony is likely to be brief, brisk, and accurate; nonetheless, many clients will giggle in an embarrassed way, and make some self-conscious joke touching on their close mortality."[36] Thus, Goffman points out that it is possible for joking and laughter to open up other possibilities, beyond the ongoing, particular framework.[37]

Another source of "another possibility" is "negative experience" (Goffman 1974, 379). Goffman suggests that 'breaking frame' is a 'negative experience' for the individual.[38] Briefly speaking, the 'negative experience' associated with breaking frame has a grotesque attraction which induces the involvement of individuals. In other words, the prospect of frame breaks, ironically and grotesquely, is a means of anchoring individuals. They are attracted to a frame even though—or actually because—the frame is on the verge of breaking, so it cannot provide individuals with comfort, stability, and relaxation, but rather, suspension, tension, and even fear. Such a 'negative experience' is often provided by novels, dramas, or movies, which are full of twists and gimmicks. The reader or audience is likely to be caught up, because of the attraction of witnessing that "precarious fabrication is soon destroyed" (Goffman 1974, 382).[39]

Yet, Goffman addresses the terrain of 'other possibility' more explicitly in reference to "a group's framework of frameworks," in other words, "its belief system and its cosmology" (1974, 27). In Goffman's eyes, such a problem is a standing academic hazard for all sociologists. Of course, some of them may face rather than avoid this tricky problem, even though it demands a deep consideration and effort (1974, 28). Most of the terrain of other possibilities is "still unexplained" (1974, 28). But for Goffman, "the unexplained is not the inexplicable" (1974, 441). Just as Goffman suggests "if a strip of activity is allowed to proceed long enough, the truth will out" (1974, 440), so the truth of the unexplained shall 'out' if we wait enough. This is what Goffman proposes in his *Frame Analysis*.

For Goffman, therefore, it can be said without exaggeration that it is rash or foolhardy to belittle or neglect the 'other possibilities,' contrasting them negatively with everyday life, the latter considered as clear, vivid, and "real enough in itself" (1974, 562). It is often argued that the domain of 'other possibilities' is unreal because it is still unexplained and unanswered, in other words, silent, but this is also true of everyday life, because a large portion of everyday life is also unexplained, as Goffman shows in his work. This fact becomes more and more apparent, especially in modern society. While Goffman looks to make fun of the reality of everyday life, he also suggests the likelihood that 'other possibilities' impinge on human reality. In the concluding chapter of *Frame Analysis*, Goffman, in fact, provides:

> The associated lore itself draws from the moral traditions of the community as found in folk tales, characters in novels, advertisements, myth, movie stars and their famous roles, the Bible, and other sources of exemplary representation. So everyday life, real enough in itself, often seems to be a laminated adumbration of a pattern or model that is itself a typification of quite uncertain realm status. (1974, 562)

He goes on to argue: "Life may not be an imitation of art, but ordinary conduct, in a sense, is an imitation of the proprieties, a gesture at the exemplary forms, and the primal realization of these ideals belongs more to make-believe than to reality" (Goffman 1974, 562).[40]

It is thus suggested that 'other possibilities,' which are distinct from and transcendent compared to human affairs, continuously penetrate human affairs as well. Creelan identifies Goffman's 'other possibility' with "the ultimate mystery of Being as the Sacred" (Creelan 1984, 694), and summarizes Goffman's core idea as follows:

> Much like the contemporary existentialists who emphasize human finitude and the mystery of Being, Goffman uses Job's increasingly open psyche as his basis for understanding that beyond nature, beyond society, and beyond the individual lies a mystery of Being that continually surpasses, indeed itself engenders the ever-

changing outlines of these other finite structures of existence. (Creelan 1984, 694)

Thus, it can be said that even though frames are inherently precarious, this precariousness can always be seen as a means of revealing some hidden truth, in other words, the possibility of an intricate connection between the human and the transcendent, either by the transcendent connecting with the human, or vice versa, through out-of-frame activity. Yet, it should be clearly noted that the frame itself is not sacred, but is only a humanly created form; they are, as Goffman calls them, "humanistically-sacred things" (1981b, 65).[41]

What then, are the implications for the frames of our everyday life? As Collins aptly indicates, Goffman naturally disguises what he is doing, rather than loudly declaring it (Collins 1980, 173; 1988, 42). However, the implications are suggested in a quotation from the *First Letter of Paul to the Corinthians* (7, 29–31) which Goffman relates in his *Frame Analysis*: "The time we live in will not last long. While it lasts, married men should be as if they had no wives; mourners should be as if they had nothing to grieve them, the joyful as if they did not rejoice; buyers must not count on keeping what they buy, nor those who use the world's wealth on using it to the full. For the whole frame of this world is passing away" (1974, 491).

What Goffman intends with this wonderfully suggestive quotation can be put simply: Do not take the frame so seriously that you are enthralled by it, but also do not try to escape from worldly frames completely.[42] Participate in the human framework, but with detached playfulness.[43] And, take your time: the truth will come out.

What has been described above is Goffman's attempt to communicate both the finitude, fragility, vagueness, and uncertainty of frameworks, and at the same time the possibility of transcendence. Even though Goffman can be considered a 'mythmaker'[44] in the sense that he emphasizes 'other possibilities' and transcendence, he is strikingly modern in the sense that he employs very modern methods to do so, namely, methods of casting suspicion and doubt upon familiar things.[45]

AGENCY

We now turn to the understanding of the self in Goffman's work. Much of the above discussion of social order had clear implications for an understanding of human agency, but I will try to be succinct and avoid redundancy in my efforts to uncover the understanding of modernity in Goffman's view of the self, or human agency.

For Goffman, the increasing uncertainty of the world is accompanied by increasing instability for the individual. In other words, the more the world becomes opaque, the more the individual becomes ambiguous. Let's look more specifically at Goffman's portrayal of the individual, with reference to modernity.

We can first consider the individual as a "sacred object" (Goffman 1967, 31). The uncertainty of the world leaves the individual to withdraw his assignment of sacredness to the outside world, and to assign this inwardly.[46] It is only the human being that is considered as sacred in modern times. In other words, the individual as a "sacred object" (1953b, 103) must be praised or worshiped as an autonomous individual god.[47] Goffman observes that:

> Durkheimian notions about primitive religion can be translated into concepts of deference and demeanor, and . . . these concepts help us to grasp some aspects of urban secular living. The implication is that in one sense this secular world is not so irreligious as we might think. Many gods have been done away with, but the individual himself stubbornly remains as a deity of considerable importance. He walks with some dignity and is the recipient of many little offerings. He is jealous of the worship due him, yet, approached in the right spirit, he is ready to forgive those who may have offended him. Because of their status relative to his, some persons will find him contaminating while others will find they contaminate him, in either case finding that they must treat him with ritual care. Perhaps the individual is so viable a god because he can actually understand the ceremonial significance of the way he is treated, and

quite on his own can respond dramatically to what is proffered him. In contacts between such deities there is no need for middlemen; each of these gods is able to serve as his own priest. (Goffman 1967, 95)

Goffman here considers ritual or rite[48] not as a constraint, but as a means of worshiping the small god, that is, the individual. The individual can be seen, therefore, as a player in a ritual game to save one's sacred face (1967, 19). Goffman speaks of "the self as a kind of player in a ritual game who copes honorably or dishonorably, diplomatically or undiplomatically, with the judgmental contingencies of the situation" (1967, 31). Here, it is the individual himself, as a small god, that maintains the situation, not the institutional order.

Next, we should discuss Goffman's notion of the individual as a weak vessel. The individual as a god is likely to be blasphemed. As Goffman notes, men as sacred objects "are subject to slights and profanation" (1967, 31). The individual might therefore commit himself to continuously monitor whether he is doing wrong to others and whether others are doing wrong to him. Goffman states that "by repeatedly and automatically asking himself the question, 'if I do or do not act in this way, will I or others lose face?' he decides at each moment, consciously or unconsciously, how to behave" (1967, 31).

The individual as a sacred object is also subject to be exploited for the egoistic interests of seeming worshipers. A succinct example is provided by mental hospitals. For Goffman, the treatment of patients in mental hospitals does not fit the medical-service model. That is, mental hospitals manipulate patients for their egoistic interests. Goffman formulated in his *Asylums:*

> ... in citing the limitations of the service model [I do not] mean to claim that I can suggest some better way of handling persons called mental patients. Mental hospitals are not found in our society because supervisors, psychiatrists, and attendants want jobs; mental hospitals are found because there is a market for them. If all the mental hospitals in a given region were emptied and closed down today, tomorrow relatives, police, and judges

would raise a clamor for new ones; and these true clients of the mental hospital would demand an institution to satisfy their needs. (1961a, 384)

Like mental patients, the "human vessel" more generally is seen as "notoriously weak" (Goffman 1961a, 177). To maintain his sacredness, the individual needs not only to make an effort himself, for example, "covering" (1963b, 102) to hide his own stigmata and prevent them from being exploited by others, but also requires the active cooperation of others. This need to constantly maintain the situation and save face can be likened to permanent reflection (Schelsky 1965).

Third, we can consider the individual as a small open city. If one understands the fragility of the self, it will not be surprising that the self is easily threatened, defeated and conquered. For Goffman, "the self is not a fortress, but rather a small open city" (1961a, 165). Whenever the self, as a small, open city, is threatened, the self is reborn. In other words, there is a consequent "process of redefining the self" (1952, 456). What is frustrating, however, is that being threatened and being born-again form a process *ad infinitum*. The individual is condemned to "regularly define" himself in terms of "a set of attributes" in every new situation (1952, 462).

Perhaps the self is threatened and reborn more often in modern society than in any other, because the modern individual lives in plural and discrepant atmospheres, and the self arises differently from each particular scene of social interaction. Goffman suggests, "[the] self itself does not derive from its possessor, but from the whole scene of his action, being generated by that attribute of local events which renders them interpretable by witnesses . . . this self—is a *product* of a scene that comes off, and is not a cause of it (1959, 252). Therefore, the self is seen as a product of social arrangements (1959, 253) which are open-ended, and vary according to the *hic et nunc*. Speaking positively, such a self is seen as a man of possibility; but speaking negatively, this is a man without qualities.

Fourth, the individual can be considered as a transcendent being. Although the self is a small open city, vulnerable to the vicissitudes of the situation, it retains some autonomy. When the individual is charged with doing something, he can nevertheless be disloyal to the particular activity. In other words, the individual can be distant from what he is doing. The individual cannot be thoroughly dissolved in the roles assigned by society.

With regard to this issue, Goffman provides us with the concept of 'role distance' (1961a, 319; 1961b, 106–7). Role distance describes a distance between an individual and a role, including the identity which accompanies a role. Role distance allows the individual leeway to accept a role in his own way, and to neglect the virtual self that is typically considered to be a part of the role. Thus, this capacity is seen as a special kind of "absenteeism" (1961a, 188), that guarantees the freedom of the self.[49] To that extent, Goffman proclaims that "whenever worlds are laid on, underlives develop" (1961a, 305). This process is referred to as 'secondary adjustment' (1961a, 54, 189). And it is almost certainly correct that role distance and secondary adjustment bring with them the possibility of transcendence. Transcendence is even encouraged by the poignant awareness that no roles can ultimately provide comfort and stability.

To sum up, in the midst of the abstraction and ambiguity of modern society, individuals turn their eyes inward. They start to search for something clear and certain within themselves. Unfortunately, they find that the self is also assailed by ambiguity and uncertainty. As soon as they think that they grasp the tangible self in the *hic et nunc*, the self evaporates. Therefore, the self also turns out to be opaque to modern man, except while in the *hic et nunc*.

What has been described above reflects well the characteristics of modern man. The individual is a stranger,[50] hovering here and there without any destination, skeptical of everything. The individual is an anonymous free-floating unit (1971, 5) facing tremendous doubts (1970, 81) in a world of fragile trust (1967, 59) with nothing but impression management (1959, 208) to assist him in his encounters with others.

This image of the individual seen in Goffman's early and middle period is sustained in his later period, though in a slightly modified way. In his *Frame Analysis*, Goffman seems to be weary of showing the fleeting, contingent nature of the self, and searches for a much more solid self, what Collins calls the "ultimate self" (1988b, 63). It should be emphasized, however, that the pursuit of the ultimate self is founded upon and starts with the free-floating nature of the self, which Goffman deliberately portrays.

Goffman sees the aimless free-floating nature of the self as an indication of the individual's search for the ultimate self. That is, for Goffman, the individual's wandering between realms of being, or frames, can be seen to have an obvious purpose: the search for the "true self" (1974, 294) or "perduring self" (1974, 293).[51] The phenomenon of role distance can be viewed, not just simply as an evasion of one's responsibility, or being aimless, but as evidence of the individual's desire to be "anchored in something beyond itself" (1974, 297).

This idea, however, appears already in Goffman's previous work. For example, in his classic work, *The Presentation of Self in Everyday Life*, Goffman is already suspicious of the self as a substantive core or essence. He states: "The self, then, as a performed character, is not an organic thing that has a specific location, whose fundamental fate is to be born, to mature, and to die; it is a dramatic effect arising diffusely from a scene that is presented, and the characteristic issue, the crucial concern, is whether it will be credited or discredited" (Goffman 1959, 252–53).

However, to arrive at a true, authentic self, some grounding is required. As Goffman notes, "without something to belong to, we have no stable self" (1961a, 320). The self sparkles in the particular moment because the particular moment possesses the temporal stability which grounds the self, *ad interim* in the *hic et nunc*. But it is hopeless to search for the true self, a more enduring, solid self, in the humanly created world[52] (i.e., frameworks), because, as we have already examined, the self is so fragile and vulnerable. The ultimate self must be sought within "other possibilities," according to Goffman's *Frame Analysis*. As we have already suggested, our human reality appears to be contiguous with other possibilities, and the borderlines even appear blurred, allowing other possibilities to impinge on human affairs.

Following from the above analysis, it can be said that Goffman understands the world as ambiguous and uncertain, despite the existence of several types of order, including institutional order, ritual order, and interaction order, and frames.[53] Prominent characteristics of modernity, especially pluralism and abstraction, are easily visible in his theory of social order and man. Goffman's man is a solitary stranger,[54] rambling here and there, between the realms of being, both physically and cognitively, craving the true self and its ground.

4

HAROLD GARFINKEL

We will now consider the relations between modernity and Garfinkel's ethnomethodology,[1] with respect to both the ethnomethodological understanding of social order and the ethnomethodological understanding of agency. Before beginning, however, two provisos are necessary.

First, even though "ethnomethodology" is Garfinkel's creation, it is by no means limited to Garfinkel's work. Ethnomethodology is widely acknowledged to be the product of a so-called "company of bastards" (Lynch 1993, 4), loosely organized around Garfinkel as the founding father of the field. From early on, ethnomethodology has been the collective endeavor of many people, now spanning three generations and four continents. So I will refer at times to the work of other ethnomethodological scholars, and conversation analysts,[2] who have pursued ethnomethodological insights and methods in different directions.

Second, Garfinkel and his colleagues might grimace at my attempt to relate their work to modernity, because they are averse to abstract theorizing.[3] However, my thesis is not that ethnomethodology and conversation analysis have a theory, even an implicit theory, of modernity. I wish to suggest here that ethnomethodology and conversation analysis have more of an affinity with modern society than pre-modern society. Moreover,

I suggest that it is rewarding to explore Garfinkel's work with reference to modernity.

SOCIAL ORDER

To pursue Garfinkel's understandings of social order, we must first look at Garfinkel's understanding of society. Let me begin with a summary of ethnomethodology made by Garfinkel: "Ethnomethodology is respecifying Durkheim's lived immortal, ordinary society, evidently, doing so by working a schedule of preposterous problems" (1996, 5).

Several critiques of Garfinkel fault him for neglecting Durkheim's aphorism; "The objective reality of social facts is sociology's fundamental principle." They charge ethnomethodology with neglecting the objective reality of society. But the above definition of ethnomethodology offered by Garfinkel belies such criticisms. From the beginning, ethnomethodology's overriding concern has been with the objective reality of society investigated by Durkheim, but radically 'respecified' (Garfinkel 2001, 6).

For Garfinkel, the immortal ordinary society is uncanny and, even "strange" (Garfinkel 1996, 8). Truly, it is an "animal" (Garfinkel and Wieder 1992, 177) or a "wonderful beast" (Garfinkel 1996, 7), since nobody, barring God, knows how the immortal ordinary society is actually put together (Garfinkel 1996, 7).

In what aspects is society strange?

First, immortal, ordinary society is neither imaginable nor suppositional, but real and actual (Garfinkel and Wieder 1992, 177; Robillard 1999, 64), although, if one tries to grasp its workings, it is "elusive." Garfinkel remarks:

> Strange? In particulars, what's so strange? What is strange is already well known and available. Consider that immortal ordinary society evidently, just in any actual case, is easily done and easily recognized with uniquely adequate competence, vulgar competence, by one and all—*and*, for all that, by one and all it is intractably hard to describe procedurally. Procedurally described, just in any actual case, it is *elusive*. Further, it is only discoverable. It is not imaginable. It cannot be imagined but is only

actually found out, and just in any actual case. The way it is done is everything it can consist of and imagined descriptions cannot capture this detail. (Garfinkel 1996, 8)

In God's silence, ordinary laypeople and sages[4] who believe themselves smarter than ordinary people, preside over the strange business of immortal ordinary society (Garfinkel 1996, 8). Through theorizing, immortal society can be made into a formidable entity, like a monolith, which works according to strict rules and laws. But such theorizing can also render society "picayunish," like a sand castle below the tide-line. Garfinkel observes, "How immortal, ordinary society is put together includes the incarnate work by formal analysts of paying careful attention to the design and administration of generic representational theorizing" (Garfinkel 1996, 8). As a result, by practicing "the privileges of the transcendental analysts and the universal observer" (Garfinkel 1996, 8), both laymen and formal analysts reject "enacted local practices" (1996, 8) as a "preposterous problem," regarding them as illogical, irrational, absurd, and a completely useless residue for explaining the immortal ordinary society. Consequently, all that remains are internal rules of theorizing itself (ranging from quantitative/statistical methods, and standards of qualitative description, to logical rules of explanation or interpretation) and the external rules of theorizing (i.e., the rules and laws posited by laymen and professionals in formal analysis). All that is left of analysis is the interpretation of the world of "signs" (1996, 8) through the analysts' own 'formulations' (Garfinkel and Sacks 1970) or 'models' (Garfinkel 1996, 7). However, by so doing, Garfinkel objects, they "lose the very phenomenon that they profess" (1996, 7). Garfinkel proclaims in a recent paper:

> The skills with which these jobs are done are everywhere accompanied by curious incongruities. These are well known, and even freely acknowledged, they include that with the same procedural skills of carrying out these jobs the phenomena they so carefully describe are lost.
>
> Further, the procedure of generic representational theorizing puts in place of the enacted witnessable detail of immortal ordinary society a collection of signs. The [formal analytic] procedure ignores the enacted, unmediated,

directly and immediately witnessable details of immortal ordinary society. Then, analysts have only one option, in order to carry through their analytic enterprises, these being the careful enterprises of description that will permit the demonstration of the corpus status of ordinary actions; in order to do *that*, analysts become interpreters of signs. Following through consistently with this procedure, it is then argued that interpretation is unavoidable. That designing and interpreting 'marks, indicators, signs, and symbols' is inevitably what sociologists and social scientists must do in order to carry out the corpus status of their studies of ordinary activities. (Garfinkel 1996, 8)

Whereas theoretical formulations or models seem quite plausible to laymen and professional theorists, ethnomethodology and conversation analysis are highly suspicious of such theorizing and its formulations and models. This is because, as Garfinkel and Sacks argue, the formulations which are designed to remedy or clarify[5] the preposterous or vague content of ordinary conversation, actually do something quite different from their intended purposes (Garfinkel and Sacks 1970, 355). That is, formulations do not simply refer to, reflect, clarify, or correct something; rather, they do much more than that. For example, in the case of an interrogatory sequence in conversation, formulations are used as a kind of hit and run device: they act as "thrusts, parries, feints, and dodges" (Lynch 1993, 186).[6]

What is more important for us here is that Garfinkel and Sacks point out that people are able to make sense of each other in stride, without doing formulation. With regard to this, Garfinkel and Sacks propose that, "We have seen that and how members do [the fact that our activities are accountably rational]. We have seen that the work is done without having to do formulations; that the terms which have to be clarified are not to be replaced by formulations that would not do what they do" (1970, 358).

Garfinkel goes on to argue that to see the immortal ordinary society requires no great sociological sophistication, theorizing and models, and that theory is incapable of producing definitive formulations.[7] Garfinkel here appears to be marching inexorably toward the terrain of preposterous problems, in other words, the "enacted local practices" (Garfinkel 1996, 8) of the "perspicuous settings" (Garfinkel and Wieder 1992, 181), considered picayune or trivial by laymen and those engaged in formal analysis. Garfinkel turns his attention to enacted local practices, and begins his exploration of immortal ordinary society with them, in order to cleanse the Augean stables. He states:

> [Ethnomethodology] is not in the business of interpreting signs. It is not an interpretive enterprise. Enacted local practices are not texts which symbolize 'meanings' or events. They are in detail identical with themselves, and not representative of something else. The witnessably recurrent details of ordinary everyday practices constitute their own reality. They are studied in their unmediated details and not as signed enterprises. (Garfinkel 1996, 8)

Garfinkel goes on to proclaim that ethnomethodological studies do not "correspond to" and "represent" social order phenomena, that they are not "interpretations" of "indicators, marks, signs, symbols, codes, or texts" (Garfinkel 2001, 6). Instead, ethnomethodological studies "exhibit" social order (Garfinkel 2001, 7).

For Garfinkel, formal analysis with its theorizing produces 'metaphysical pictures' (Lynch 1993, 218), while deprecating and excluding the enacted local practices from its research. Garfinkel and his colleagues are not convinced by these analytical formulations, but they go about their business "without disputing" and "without sacrificing" (1996, 6–7) the achievements of formal analysis. After all, formal analysis is a feature of immortal society, and disputing its achievements could therefore involve analytical formulations of features of ordinary society.[8] "No disrespect is involved for [formal analysis's] demand that its investigations be worldly work of finding out and specifying real order, evidently; real order, not cockamamie real order. Real order is [formal analysis's] achievement, without question. [Ethnomethodology] is not claiming to know better" (Garfinkel 1996, 6).[9]

Be this as it may, Garfinkel's ethnomethodology avoids the instructably observable phenomena (Garfinkel 1996, 5) of social order investigated by formal analysis, proceeding directly to naturally occurring activities.

In studying these enacted local practices, ethnomethodology focuses on the "constitutive features" (Garfinkel 1959, 54) of activities, which are (to recall an earlier phrase from Garfinkel) "seen but unnoticed."[10] This focus requires ethnomethodology to be fully attentive to everything that is going on. It seems to be a strikingly difficult task, precisely because it has to "catch the work of 'fact production' in flight" (Garfinkel 1967a, 79).[11] Moreover, it involves attempting to unfamiliarize the familiar. Ethnomethodology gives priority to the "procedures" according to which everything occurs (Garfinkel 1996, 6). Garfinkel calls it the quest of "What More" (1996, 6), noting:

> Ethnomethodology... is proposing and working out 'What More' there is to the unquestionable corpus status of formal analytic investigations than formal analysis does, did, ever did, or can provide.... [ethnomethodology] asks 'What More' is there that users of formal analysis know and demand the existence of, that [formal analysis] depends upon the existence of for [formal analysis] worksite-specific achievements in carefully instructed procedures, that [formal analysis] uses and recognizes everywhere in and as its lived worksite-specific practices. (Garfinkel 1996, 6)

He goes on to point out that "'What More' has centrally (and perhaps entirely) to do with procedures.... By *procedural*, [ethnomethodology] does not mean *process*. Procedural means labor.... At the worksite—progressively and developingly coming upon the phenomenon via the work in and as of the unmediated details of producing it" (Garfinkel 1996, 6).[12]

Consequently, ethnomethodology is able to apprehend phenomena without any presuppositions or prejudices (which are central to formal analysis) by merely searching for "What More" under particular circumstances (Garfinkel 1996, 6). Garfinkel elsewhere likens this task to "extracting an animal from the foliage" (Garfinkel, Lynch, and Livingston 1981, 132). The 'foliage' is the "local historicity" of members' enacted embodied activities within particular worksites or "perspicuous settings" (Garfinkel and Wieder 1992, 184).[13] The 'animal' is that "local history is done, recognized, and understood as a competent methodic procedure" (Garfinkel, Lynch, and Livingston 1981, 132). The animal refers to members' embodiedly witnessable local competent activities as displaying "transcendental properties" (Garfinkel, Lynch, and Livingston 1981, 132) of various settings of immortal ordinary society. In order to extract the animal from the foliage, a ceaseless effort must be made to enter, start, and end "in the midst of things" (Garfinkel 1996, 6). As Garfinkel proposes: "We'll proceed without having to decide or even to know how to proceed while knowing nothing. Instead, by [beginning], by [carrying on], by [finding our bearings again], by [completing an investigation] we'll land ourselves in the midst of *things*... In the midst of... endless things we'll study the work as of which immortal ordinary society consists. We'll see" (Garfinkel 1996, 6).

There are two fundamental reasons why Garfinkel and his colleagues attend to spates of naturally occurring activities. The reasons are inextricably interlocked with the problem of social order. First of all, according to ethnomethodology and conversation analysis, there is order in the "plenum" (Garfinkel 1996, 7), despite its appearance as a disordered, preposterous problem. Garfinkel argues that the proponents of formal analysis seek order in their theorizing, and claim there is no order in the concrete activities of the plenum. However, Garfinkel observes an order evident "in the concreteness of things" (1996, 7). To adopt an earlier observation of Harvey Sacks, "there is order at all points" (Sacks 1984, 22), even in trivial and schlock settings.[14] Put differently, naturally occurring activities are equipped with the "orderliness of practical action" (Livingston 1987, 12).

Garfinkel formulates:

> ... there is order in the most ordinary activities of everyday life in their full concreteness, and that means in their ongoingly procedurally enacted coherence of substantive, ordered phenomenal details without loss of generality. It has to do with the unexplicated specifics of details in structures, in recurrencies, in typicality, not the details gotten by administering a generic description. These

details are unmediatedly experienced and experienced evidently. (Garfinkel 1996, 7)

Within such arguments, ethnomethodology's concepts of 'order' and 'structure' become modified and extended, and become highly distinct from those of formal analysis. Firstly, for Garfinkel, structure is conceived as visible recurrencies of ordinary activities as omnipresent achievements,[15] rather than as macro phenomena, as in formal analysis.[16] Thus, all repetitive or regular patterns of practical activities are regarded as structures, even the most trivial. In this connection, Garfinkel states:

> Without sacrificing issues of structure or changing the subject? That means without sacrificing the ubiquitous achievements, in everyday life, of recognizable and accountable, observable recurrencies of practical actions and practical reasoning in achievedly coherent, ordered, uniquely adequate details of generality, of comparability, of classification, of typicality, of uniformity, of standardization. These are recurrencies in productions of the phenomena of ordinary activities—traffic jams, service lines, summoning phones, blackboard notes, jazz piano in a cocktail lounge, talking chemistry in lecture format—phenomena that *exhibit*, along with their other endogenously accountable details, the endogenously accountable populations that staff their production. (Garfinkel 1996, 7)[17]

With regard to the conception of order, one can discern equally significant differences between Garfinkel's ethnomethodology and formal analysis. To indicate the difference between the conventional notion of order and his own, Garfinkel adds an asterisk: 'order*'. Whereas 'order' refers to the ordinary usage in formal analysis, 'order*' as recently invoked by Garfinkel[18] indicates the all-embracing order ostensibly observable, witnessable, and discoverable, regarding the practical activities of members. This includes the formal order discussed by conventional formal analysis. As Garfinkel and Wieder describe it, "order* is a collector and a proxy for any and every topic of logic, meaning, method, reason, and order. It stands in for any and all the marvelous topics that are available in received lingoes and studies in the endless arts and sciences of practical action" (1992, 202).

Garfinkel offers a much more important contribution to the study of order, however, than the notarization, rediscovery or inclusion of a neglected variety of order.[19] This contribution, or "respecification" (1991, 10), to use Garfinkel's term, is that any kind of order, whether 'order'' or 'order,' is "locally produced" (Garfinkel and Wieder 1992, 203) by the "endogenous population" (Garfinkel 1996, 5) at the particular moment. Put differently, if order is seen as a live–observable–witnessable "animal," there is no way of capturing order outside of the ordinary practical activities of the endogenous population: there would be only a fossil which could never be animated. Garfinkel and Wieder comment:

> Do not think, however, that Ethnomethodology seeks out these creatures in order to settle with them as topics of order*. Nothing of the sort. Rather, [ethnomethodology] seeks to respecify them as locally produced, naturally accountable phenomena of order*. . . . We shall understand any of the topics of order* as locally produced, naturally accountable phenomena, searched for, findable, found, only discoverably the case, consisting in and as 'work of the streets.' (1992, 203)

From non-ethnomethodological, conventional, perspectives, not only can Garfinkel's notion of order be seen as the order of the uninteresting, but ethnomethodologists can be seen as sociological 'schlockmeisters.'

Now, to introduce the problem of modernity. The discovery or rediscovery of order within practical activities must be considered encouraging news for those concerned with modern man, *pace* Garfinkel's dislike of theorizing. The traditional, institutional, macro order is attenuated, but there is new-found order intrinsically immanent in man's ordinary practical activities, an order which could provide modern man with the desired predictability, stability and certainty. What this means can be put quite simply: there is some stability for modern man, *faute de mieux*, who suffers from "permanent reflection" (Schelsky [1959] 1987; 1965), and "de-institutionalization" (Gehlen

1956; cf. Berger 1980). It could even be argued that the order rediscovered by Garfinkel is in some ways more basic and more important than traditional conceptions of order. The order Garfinkel wants to explicate and respecify is of greater advantage *facile princeps*, even though it exists in human affairs *ab initio*.

As Thomas Scheff (1990) observes, in modern times, people, even professional sociologists, find it harder and harder to observe "recurring patterns in the macro world." Since this world is so abstract and "so vast," it may require special techniques and tools to "make its regularities visible" (1990, 27).

This observation raises the question of whether it is completely coincidental that Garfinkel's understanding of structure as locally produced appears when society is at the height of abstraction. It is certainly reasonable to suspect that ethnomethodology's innovative conception of structure is related to the abstract nature of traditional structure in modern society.

Importantly, the order attended to by Garfinkel, as John Heritage (1984) aptly points out, is not "top-down," but "from the bottom up" (1984, 83–4).[20] More precisely, it is endogenous,[21] not exogenous, order: "in, about, as and over the course of the *in vivo*" (Garfinkel and Wieder 1992, 203).[22] As Garfinkel points out, "these phenomena are locally and endogenously produced, naturally organized, reflexively accountable in and as of details, and therein they provide for everything that details could possibly be" (1991, 16–17).

There is another reason why Garfinkel limits himself to the order of ordinary practical activities; Garfinkel believes that every order, even the macro/institutional order, or the order of formal analysis, begins and ends with ordinary practical activities. Thus, for Garfinkel, one cannot understand the problem or the nature of the macro/institutional order without approaching it from within ordinary practical activities. Ethnomethodology, therefore, argues that institutional/macro order or phenomena cannot be considered 'self-subsistent entities' (Heritage 1984, 229), independent of the ordinary practical activities of members. From the perspective of ethnomethodology, speaking of the institutional order without specifying how-and-that it arises in the situated activities of members, amounts to reifying the institutional order.

To avoid reifying 'macro structures,' ethnomethodology rigorously investigates the endogenous population's methods of discovering, for example, 'really what they are doing,' by which methods the institutional order is constructed (Hilbert 1990, 796).[23] Therefore, for Garfinkel and his colleagues, the institutional order is nothing but an "occasioned corpus," a temporally situated "achievement" of members to a specific setting (Zimmerman and Pollner 1970, 94).[24]

With regard to the issue of institutional order, and especially macro-structural phenomena, Garfinkel proposes:

> Structural phenomena such as income and occupational distributions, familial arrangements, class strata, and the statistical properties of language are emergent products of a vast amount of communicative, perceptual, judgmental, and other "accommodative" work whereby persons, in concert, and encountering "from within the society" the environments that the society confronts them with, establish, maintain, restore, and alter the social structures that are the assembled products of temporally extended courses of action directed to these environments as persons "know" them. (1963, 187–8)

Under the rubric of Garfinkel's original formulation, Jeff Coulter (1982; 1996a; 2001) is greatly elucidating the problem of macro phenomena by extending the study of "membership categorization practices," initiated by Harvey Sacks.[25] According to Coulter, "the panoply of social configurations," which are identified by laymen and professionals as macro-structural phenomena such as institutions, organizations or society as a whole, can only be "encountered" or invoked in and through members' "practical activities of looking, describing, inferring from parts to wholes, categorizing, abstracting, following rules and the rest" (Coulter 1982, 34).

Therefore, macro-structural phenomena are describable and analyzable in terms of members' categorization practices. As a result, if we see how members use "collectivity-categorizations" (Coulter 1982, 37) such as 'states,' 'nations,' 'class,' 'army,' 'government,' 'university,' and so on, we can arrive at the precise nature of "their ontological status" (1982, 41). Neither considering macro phenomena as self-subsistent entities, nor as Coulter puts it, "labels for unambiguously given objects" (1982, 41), nor as any sort of "container" (1982, 43; 1996a, 9), nor as events necessarily being committed in "large number" (1996a, 10), Coulter considers them to be temporarily animated, visualized, invoked, produced, accomplished, sustained, situated, localized, and done by means of members' activities. [26] In other words, he rejects all 'decontextualized' (1982, 40) understandings of macro phenomena.

In his "Remarks on the Conceptualization of Social Structure," Coulter proclaims: "In producing and giving accounts of activities so mundanely describable, we are as members thereby also furnishing the presupposed organizations and institutions with their life: we are in these ways constituting them, for they obtain their real-worldly character from such instantiations" (1982, 44). And, in a similar vein, Coulter remarks elsewhere:

> Under specific ranges of circumstances, when certain persons do and/or say specific sorts of things according to specific rules (rules constituting also under what identification auspices their conduct is to be construed), these cases instantiate the conduct of macro-phenomena. They bring these phenomena to life, they realize them, in occasioned ways, such that they (again, recurrently) enter into our lives as part of our structures of relevant orientation. [27] (1996a, 11)

Within the context of Coulter's arguments, it could be suggested that macro social phenomena might be seen as no more than a members' sense, [28] which they use or manipulate to justify, explain, describe, excuse, or make sense of their ordinary activities. What is of greatest significance here is that only while the members are instantiating macro categories do macro social configurations appear and exist *ad interim* in the *hic et nunc*.

To introduce some remarks on modernity here, it can be said without exaggeration that macro phenomena and macro order lose their intimidating stature and begin to seem very weak, according to this analysis. Put differently, the picture invoked by ethnomethodology here suggests that the macro institutional social order, which once appeared to determine behavior, now no longer impinges on it at all. Nor have macro phenomena taken members in tow, nor trampled members under foot; on the contrary, members construct macro order. The foundation of macro phenomena, after all, is in members' ordinary practical activities *in situ*.

Macro phenomena now flash in and out of existence with the orientations and illocutions of members. That is, the "localization of phenomena" (Sharrock and Anderson 1986, 92) can flame out in a moment. As Coulter states, "In particular, an adequate appreciation of the role of the 'macro-order' in our everyday lives reveals that such phenomena are variously instantiated in what we say and do and also that our conduct is by no means omnirelevantly linked to 'macro-level' considerations" (1996a: 22).

What is of much greater interest for us here is this: it is hardly a coincidence that ethnomethodology's approach to the macro order emphasizes features that are most easily observed in modernity. In fact, there is a startling resemblance between the two. I am not claiming that the ethnomethodological view is determined or historically relative, only that there is a definite affinity between the ethnomethodological view and major features of modern society.

The macro order is threatened even more by two facts of human behavior illustrated by ethnomethodology. These are the ingrained ambiguity of human activities, and the looseness between human behaviors and rules (and norms), in other words, the indeterminacy of rules and of norms. These features of human practices show the touch-and-go nature of all human orders.

Firstly, we can mention the inherent indexicality of human activities (Garfinkel 1967a, 34). Both Garfinkel and Sacks are conscious of the intrinsic ambiguity of human practices and expressions.[29] In Garfinkel's work, he discovers that the world-taken-for-granted is replete with ambiguity and vagueness *in nucleo*.[30] Furthermore, as we remarked above with reference to formal analysis, the world taken-for-granted would disappear if one attempted to expunge all ambiguity.

The view that human conduct is intrinsically uncertain could be understood as a source of alarm, but according to Garfinkel, members don't give up in the face of ambiguity and uncertainty,[31] rather they *trade* on ambiguity.[32] Members have an "actual light," as Garfinkel writes in his Ph.D. dissertation (1952, 116), which allows them to work through, even exploit ambiguity. There is "stable" (Lynch 1993, 21) and clear meaning temporarily adumbrated and created by members' own activities. It is an arcanum of human activities, and Garfinkel calls it "the demonstrably rational properties" of human activities (Garfinkel 1967a, 34).

Therefore, the primary concern of ethnomethodology is with the manner in which members manage to make sense *ad rem* and attain order *ad interim* with any available resources or devices in whatever particular circumstances.[33] This is hinted at in Garfinkel's observation, "much that is being talked about is not mentioned, although each expects that the adequate sense of the matter being talked about is settled" (1963, 221).

In this connection, social order for Garfinkel refers to the ongoing "contingent achievements of organizations of common practices" (1967a, 33) by members, using whatever resources "there are to hand to get done the tasks and business they are engaged in" (Hester and Eglin 1997, 1).[34]

In the teeth of inherent uncertainty, "ambiguity and equivocality" (Garfinkel 1967b, 173), members can rely upon a temporal, contingent certainty, good for all practical purposes, at least, mastering mundane interaction as unproblematically meaningful. Of course, it should be clearly noted here again that the problem of whether the certainty is grounded is not the concern for ethnomethodology and conversation analysis. Ethnomethodologists and conversational analysts are inexorably indifferent to the problem. Rather, the only concern of ethnomethodology is to investigate how members construct and sustain the sense of certainty in and through their concerted activities under particular circumstances.

The tendency to rush toward certainty and stability,[35] or toward what Rawls calls "the preference orders" (1989b, 162), is not only satisfied in the orderliness of practical activities, but this orderliness of practical activities also establishes and instantiates order with all the appearance of a *fait accompli*, in and through the contingently and temporarily concerted alignments of members' practical activities. To that extent, one can plausibly argue that ethnomethodology's trenchant discoveries of the nature of social order, in other words, order embedded in the ambiguity, equivocality, contingency, and temporality of interaction,[36] may well be a reflection of especially modern phenomena.

Another fundamental dimension of the contingency of order in ethnomethodology comes from the indeterminacy of rules (and norms) for human conduct. It is widely held that rules and norms are determinate and help constitute a solid order. However, Garfinkel decisively challenges the notion that members strictly toe the line, and that their conduct is determined by rules and norms. As Heritage (1984, 34) aptly notes, Garfinkel rejects the so-called rule-governed model.

How, then, does Garfinkel understand rules?

First of all, in Garfinkel's eyes, rules do not completely, exhaustively cover the full range of possible conduct. Even in a simple game, the fact that rules cannot completely govern all possible conduct can be easily demonstrated. [37] Secondly, in addition, even specific and explicit rules which pertain to a particular event are essentially vague and fail to determinately specify the manner of their own application. [38] Consequently, no matter how clear and explicit the rule may appear, there would remain an empty space it could not occupy. Ambiguity, equivocality and obscurity would remain extant in members' activities, which are only possible by means of a practical competence which is inherently extemporaneous and *ad hocing*. (Garfinkel 1967b, 173–4). Garfinkel adds:

> I am not giving you a genetic account. I am not giving you a causal account of rule following. I am trying to give a production account. I am trying to ask: when a person seems to be following rules, what is it that that seems to consist of? We need to describe how it gets done. These practices of etc., unless, let it pass, the pretense of agreeing, the use of sanctioned vagueness, the waiting for something later to happen which promises to clarify what has gone before, the avoidance of monsters even when they occur and the borrowing of exceptions are all involved. I am proposing these as practices whereby persons make what they are doing happen as rule-analyzable conduct. (1968, 220)

Finally, there is a more fundamental logic to the limitations of rules. Limitations allow for the transformability of rules across cases. Briefly speaking, rules must, as Heritage points out, "be applied, and to specific configurations of circumstances which may never be identical" (1984, 121). To use Garfinkel's phrase, rules are always trying to catch up with ever-changing circumstances. Yet, rules continue in their application to activities despite the fact that they never apply absolutely. [39]

To sum up some of the above considerations, there are no rules that can be seen as determining members' conduct in any straightforward sense, *tout a fait*. There are no clear-cut-all-embracing rules. Rules remain in the terrain of ambiguity, they are followed by means of the exquisite, complicated, tacit competence of members.

Therefore, members are not imprisoned in a dungeon of rules. Rather, rules achieve their reality in and through their invocations by members. One of the most succinct examples of this is suggested by Wieder (1974; 1988), in his study of a deviant subculture in a halfway house. Wieder encounters "the code"—a tacit moral system which identifies activities that residents "should and should not engage in" (1974, 140), such as: 'Do not snitch,' 'Do not cop out,' 'Do not take advantage of other residents,' 'Share what you have,' 'Help other residents,' 'Do not mess with other resident's interests,' 'Do not trust staff—staff is heat,' and 'Show your loyalty to the residents' (Wieder 1974, 145–7).

Wieder observes that the code (the collection of rules) is simply the fact that residents and staff describe, explain, avoid, and justify the actions in such a way. Put differently, Wieder finds out that the code is employed as a sense-making, an accounting, and a persuasive device. [40] Wieder provides:

> . . . [the code] was a device for legitimately declining a suggestion or order. It was a device for urging or defeating a proposed course of action. It was a device for accounting for why one should feel or act in the way that one did as an expectable, understandable, reasonable, and above all else acceptable way of acting or feeling. It was, therefore, a way of managing a course of conversation in such a way as to present the teller (or his

colleague) as a reasonable, moral, and competent fellow. The code, then, is much more a *method* of moral persuasion and justification than it is a substantive account of an organized way of life. It is a way, or set of ways, of causing activities to be seen as morally, repetitively, and constrainedly organized. (Wieder 1974, 158)

Wieder adds: "It is much more appropriate to think of the code as a continuous, ongoing process, rather than as a set of stable elements of culture which endure through time" (1974, 161).

By invoking and referring to rules, members can not only describe, explain, excuse, and justify their own course of actions,[41] but can also appeal to rules' law-like façade. Therefore, for ethnomethodology the relationship between rules and members may be seen as a *mariage de convenance* at best, not one of submission. Ethnomethodology's conception of rule, incorporating ambiguity, obscurity, vagueness, contingency, and indeterminacy undermines any conception of social order as enduring, stable, and determinate. In other words, the contingency and temporality of rules is a central finding of ethnomethodology.

As ethnomethodology has developed, Garfinkel has become more and more original in his understanding of rules. Whereas in his early days[42] Garfinkel rejected normative rules in favor of "invariant" rules (1954) (or "prominent rules" [1959, 57], or "basic rules" [1963, 190]), the latter day Garfinkel appears to abandon the pursuit of rules in any form. Indeed, basic rules had been regarded as the *sine qua non* for "the constitutive order" (Garfinkel 1963, 194), because they "provide a behavior's sense as an action" (1963, 195). It was considered to be a real normative rule *ab intra*. Most ethnomethodologists and conversational analysts have devoted themselves to finding such basic rules. The latter day Garfinkel rejects such efforts, because such efforts could give the impression that ethnomethodology and conversation analysis are preoccupied with these newly found rules, especially to those who believe in stable and invariant normative rules.[43] Put differently, Garfinkel doesn't want to appear to be playing to the gallery.

However, there is a much more fundamental reason why Garfinkel is set against the pursuit of basic rules, as well as, needless to say, normative rules; The preoccupation with basic rules is likely to fail to capture the embodied work of members, by diluting the "*ad hocing* practices" (Garfinkel 1967a, 21) of the *hic et nunc* (1967a, 68).

According to Lynch (1993) and Livingston (1987, 85), Garfinkel's abhorrence of the pursuit of rules as pre-given or context-free forces him to re-examine the latter day conversation analysis. [44] Indeed, Garfinkel and some of his colleagues are suspicious of and critical of the tendency of the latter-day conversation analysts to "consolidate" (Lynch 1993, 232) their findings into a "machinery, mechanism, device, apparatus and system" (Lynch 1993, 228), including basic rules governing how conversationalists talk (e.g., the 'turn taking system' [Sacks, Schegloff, and Jefferson 1974] and the 'adjacency pair' [Schegloff and Sacks 1974]), and including rules governing how members describe persons (e.g., 'membership categorization,' including the 'economy rule,' and the 'consistency rule,' [Sacks 1974]). The attempts of conversation analysis to isolate basic rules can be easily observed. [45] The following argument by Wilson is illustrative: "the fundamental mechanisms of interaction are the tools members of society use to construct their interaction. These mechanisms, while context sensitive, are context-free and so are not socially constructed in the same sense. Rather, they are universally available devices employed by members in that work of construction" (1991, 26).

Garfinkel therefore rejects the latter-day conversation analysis' emphasis on a "context-free 'core' of rules, norms, and other social structure" (Lynch 1993, 272). Garfinkel and his colleagues appear to abandon an *ad captandum* attempt to provide a context-free, stable core, and reject any structure made of or defined by any kind of "general set of rules or mechanism" (Lynch, 1993, 280), whether the rules are *ab intra* or *ab extra*, and head for the wilderness. [46] Garfinkel and his colleagues focus instead on an open-ended array of extemporaneous "artful practices" (Garfinkel 1967a, 32; 1967b, 174), with "*ad hoc* consideration" (1967a, 21), that can take "innumerable forms." Garfinkel is interested in nothing save the manner in which members' artful practices make something "immortal" "in and as of the just thisness [*haecceities*]" (Garfinkel 1996, 10) of the *hic et nunc*. Garfinkel's program excludes *tout a fait* consideration of the "fat moment" (Garfinkel 1952, 147) [47] and 'stable core meaning' (Lynch 1993, 284).

Consequently, "the just thisness" of an object, or, haecceity, hinges on the *hic et nunc*. The 'just thisness' is only clear "*in situ*" (Garfinkel et al. 1981, 133) and only the "first time through" (1981, 134). That is, as soon as the clarity of the 'just thisness' flickers *in situ*, it is lost in a maze of aeonian ambiguity. With regard to this, Lynch states that "the just thisness of an object can include the accountable here-and-now presence of a 'this' or 'it' that does not already stand for a named and verifiable thing" (1993, 284).

Nothing is fixed, stable, unchanged, or the same. We can take the example of a baseball game in Fenway Park. Every game has different players, a different audience, different weather conditions, different baseballs, different field conditions, different trajectories, different hotdogs and beer, and so on. An immortal 'just thisness' of baseball emerges just *in situ*, the first time through, but the 'just thisness' of tomorrow's game is not the same; it is 'another next first time.'

We can here quote at full length Garfinkel's characterization of the haecceities of immortal society, visible in freeway traffic:

> *Immortal* is borrowed from Durkheim as a metaphor for any witnessable local setting whose parties are doing some human job that can range in scale from a hallway greeting to a freeway traffic jam where there is *this* to emphasize about them: Their production is staffed by parties to a standing crap game. Of course the jobs are not games, let alone a crap game. Think of freeway flow in Los Angeles. For the cohort of drivers there, just this gang of them, driving, making traffic together, are *some*how, smoothly and unremarkably, concerting the driving to be *at* the lived production of the flow's just thisness: familiar, ordinary, uninterestingly, observably in and as observances doable and done again, and always, only, entirely in detail for everything that detail could be. In and as of the just thisness (the *haecceities*) of driving's details, just this staff are doing again just what in concert with vulgar competence they *can* do, for each another next first time; and it is this of what they are doing, that makes up the details of just that

traffic flow: That although it is of their doing, and as of the flow they are "witnessably oriented by" and "seeably directed to the production of it," they treat the organizational *thing* as of their doing, as of their own doing, but *not* of their very own, singular, distinctive authorship. And further, for just this cohort, it will be that after they exit the freeway others will come after them to do again the same familiar *things* that they—just they— *just these of us as drivings doings* are in concert doing.

Immortal is used to speak of human jobs as of which local members, being in the midst of organizational *things*, know, of just *these* organizational things they are in the midst of, that it preceded them and will be there after they leave. It is a metaphor for the great recurrencies of ordinary society, staffed, provided for, produced, observed and observable, locally and accountably in and as of an 'assemblage of haecceities.' (Garfinkel 1996, 10–11)

From the above discussion, the reader may appreciate the picture of social order that Garfinkel draws. To sum up and show how Garfinkel's ethnomethodology relates to the problem of modernity, I repeat what I noted before about social order in Garfinkel's ethnomethodology. The artful practices of members *in situ* are the ivory gate to social order, because it is through the gate of artful practices that all social order is displayed, visualized and instantiated. For Garfinkel, *mutatis mutandis*, the social order is temporary, contingent, and momentary, like the flash of fireworks in the night sky—the dark sky of ambiguity.

With regard to the problem of modernity, Garfinkel's notion of social order appears to be perfectly in tune with modernity. Garfinkel's emphasis on the *hic et nunc* seems to reflect the modern condition especially well. One could even say that the modern condition is reflexively intensified by Garfinkel's ethnomethodology, because ethnomethodology further undermines belief in certainty and stability. Furthermore, Garfinkel's arguments against the possibility of a '*Lebenswelt* pair' are especially relevant here. [48] A 'pair' in this context refers to a relationship of identity, a one-to-one correspondence, between an order of fact and the product of human activities (the 'lived work of proving'), which aim at representing this order of fact. Such a 'pair' is possible in mathematics, according to Garfinkel, but is impossible in regard to the relationship between the order of mundane interaction and accounts of this order, lay or professional (i.e., social-scientific).

Such an understanding of social order suggests that it is rather like fireworks,[49] that it is a series of contingent productions, grounded on nothing. Our social world is humanly created, and exists only in the process of creation. Social order is *experienced* as formidable and massive, despite its inherent contingency, temporality, and ephemeral nature, because order is ongoingly produced by and evident in members' activities, and because these activities, unlike fireworks, never cease.

AGENCY

Now let us look at how ethnomethodology's notion of agency relates to the problem of modernity. This task will be somewhat easier, because the above discussion of social order touches indirectly on the problem of human agency. Two dimensions of agency, namely 'self' and 'identity,' can be understood as having properties similar to those of social order noted above, especially the properties of contingency and temporality.

Among the ethnomethodological studies of agency, Garfinkel's case study of Agnes, a transsexual, is well known as an illustrative example of his studies (1967a). Before we survey ethnomethodology's notion of agency, we should first examine what Garfinkel contributes to the analysis of identity in his study of Agnes.

Garfinkel's concern is with how Agnes 'passed' as a normal female despite the continuous risk that she would be revealed as a transsexual. His study of Agnes shows us a totally different picture of gender identity than the biological approach, or role theory. For Garfinkel, Agnes is viewed as a practical methodologist, because Agnes is extremely sensitive to the details of passing as a normal female in particular situations. Unlike the common lay and sociological views of gender identity, which assume either that normal sexuality is a stable, inherent property of the individual or that it arises out of socialization, Garfinkel views sexuality as a practical and ongoing accomplishment of members through their practical activities. The sense of a stable or normal sexual identity is continually produced by activity, such as Agnes was concerned to master. Garfinkel says, "for Agnes, stable routines of everyday life were 'disengageable' attainments assured by unremitting, momentary, situated courses of improvisation" (1967a, 184).

For Garfinkel, the practices of 'passing' are not solely the prerogative of transsexuals such as Agnes. They are also used by those who try to maintain any identity, unconventional or conventional. Garfinkel himself confesses that he is also continuously trying to pass with Agnes as if he had an adequate medical knowledge. Garfinkel writes:

> Agnes' case instructs us on how intimately tied are "value stability," "object constancy," "impression management," "commitments to compliance with legitimate expectancies," "rationalization," to member's unavoidable work of coming to terms with practical circumstances. It is with respect to that phenomenon that in examining Agnes' passing I have been concerned with the question of how, over the temporal course of their actual engagements, and "knowing" the society only from within, members produce stable, accountable practical activities, i.e., social structures of everyday activities. (1967a, 185)

In other words, passing practices are not restricted to deviant cases, for example, involving transsexualism, but accompany all roles or identities. In his detailed case study of Agnes, Garfinkel finds some significant features of social interaction, such as passing practices, the achievement of identities, the importance of 'trust', and so on (Benson and Hughes 1983). Such features of social interaction can be applied beyond deviant cases, to everyone.

From Garfinkel's classic and typically detailed study of Agnes, we can grasp some of ethnomethodology's basic and idiosyncratic approach to agency.

Firstly, we can discuss self/identity in action and the self as an achievement. From the perspectives of ethnomethodology and conversation analysis, human agency is not a property of "man-in-the-sociologist's-society" (Garfinkel 1967a, 68), but of actors in practical activities. Put differently, ethnomethodology attempts to look at agency released from the dungeon of formal analysis. Therefore, for ethnomethodology, agency can never be understood as a property of a "cultural dope" or "judgmental dope" (1967a, 68). Ethnomethodology claims that agency should be examined by virtue of practical activities. For ethnomethodology and conversation analysis, agency may be seen as something which emerges, is maintained, and finally, fades way in the course of interaction *in situ*.

Concomitantly, human agency, especially identity, as Zimmerman points out, is treated as an element of the context of interaction (1998, 87). By proposing the notion of "identity-as-context," Zimmerman distinguishes three types of identities: 'discourse identities,' 'situational identities,' and 'transportable identities' (1998, 90–95). According to Zimmerman, 'discourse identities' hinge on the moment–by–moment organization of the interaction. Thus, 'discourse identities' are determined by 'what individuals are doing interactionally in a particular spate of talk' (Zimmerman 1998, 92). Examples can be drawn from relational pairs such as speaker/hearer, caller/answerer, and story teller/recipient. 'Situational identities' are specified within a broader neighborhood of types of situation, for example, emergency telephone calls, pharmacist/customer calls, or department of registrar teller/student calls. Yet, such situations can effectively play a role in constituting situational identities only when members orient to elements of the situation as significant, that is, only when participants are "engaging in activities and respecting agendas that display an orientation to, and an alignment of, particular identity sets" (Zimmerman 1998, 90). Finally, 'transportable identities' refer to "latent" identities which are carried "across situations and are potentially relevant in and for any situation and in and for any spate of interaction" (1998, 90), e.g., life-stage, sex and race. In his paper, Zimmerman confines his attention to the first two identities, that is, discourse and situational identities. But he mentions that transportable identities cannot be seen as stable core entities fixed to persons, but rather as expedients invoked for "locating and apprehending" people (Zimmerman 1998, 91).

At any rate, in conversation analysis, identities are inherently moment-based. To that extent, one might say that conversation analysts conceive of persons as "armatures of context-free and context-sensitive machineries" (Lynch 1993, 258). Persons are sentenced to continuously change their armor, from situation to situation, moment to moment. This understanding of man can be compared to the image of modern man as lacking qualities.

Ethnomethodology and conversation analysis, therefore, decline mentalist or decontextualized approaches to self/identity. [50] For ethnomethodology and conversation analysis, self and identity come into play within spates of activities within particular circumstances. The self is a "transparent, publicly-available phenomenon, a feature of social-interactional organization: no more and no less" (Watson 1998, 215), not an inner-private-mental thing (Watson 1998, 217). [51] The transparent, public and entirely manifest self or identity is possible only within the trajectory of interaction, in which participants "exhibit their *in situ* understandings of the 'here and now' of their interaction" (Watson 1998, 208).

Consequently, for ethnomethodology and conversation analysis, decontextualized approaches to self or identity, which attempt to grasp the nature of self or identity without consideration of context or the *hic et nunc*, are understood as reifying self or identity. Watson likens such approaches to searching for a chimera (1998, 215).

In sum, according to ethnomethodology and conversation analysis, the self is ongoingly achieved, produced, managed, sustained, displayed, situated, and instantiated in and through members' practical activities.

Next, we can discuss self/identity as a tool. Ethnomethodologists, and especially Harvey Sacks, the founder of conversation analysis, approach issues of self/identity in terms of membership categorization. Sacks defines membership categories as classifications and social types that members use in order to describe themselves and others, such as, 'teenager,' 'doctor,' 'mom,' 'American,' or 'baseball player.' Membership categories often interlock with others to form collections or membership categorization devices. [52] For example, 'dad,' 'mom,' and 'child' can be seen as categories from the membership category device 'family.'

Sacks proposes two rules of membership categorization: the economy rule and the consistency rule. The economy rule refers to the fact that when one describes a person one should eschew unnecessarily complicated category-using (Sacks 1974, 219); "adequate reference" to a person can be accomplished with only one categorization. Second, the consistency rule: "if some population of persons is being categorized, and if a category from some device's collection has been used to categorize a first member of the population, then that category or other categories of same collection may be used to categorize further members of the population" (1974, 219). For instance, if a person is categorized as 'first baseman,' any team-members are likely to be categorized as 'outfielder,' 'pitcher,' and so on, even though it might also be true that they are men, Christians, democrats, and so on.

Sacks also suggests a 'hearer's maxim,' which is, "if two or more categories are used to categorize two or more members of some population, and those categories can be heard as categories from the same collection, then: hear them that way" (1974, 219–20). We can refer to Sack's famous example: "The baby cried. The mommy picked it up" (Sacks 1974, 216; 1992, 236–59). Here, the incumbents of the two categories 'baby' and 'mommy' are normally and commonsensically heard as members of the same family.

For the moment, however, two points should be noted: Firstly, for ethnomethodology and conversation analysis, as Antaki and Widdicombe (1998) aptly point out, the primary concern is to see "how people use categorical work (which might include ascription, display, hinting, and leakage), not to judge "whether someone truly 'had' this or that identity category, or what 'having' that identity made them do or feel" (1998, 2). Put differently, ethnomethodologists and conversation analysts hold to 'ethnomethodological indifference' in respect to this issue of 'true' identity.

Secondly, some ethnomethodologists object to speaking of newly found rules, such as the hearer's maxim or consistency rules, that are broader than specific situations and embodied work *in situ*. Sacks, as Hester and Eglin (1997) cogently indicate, runs the risk of considering membership categorization as a somewhat "pre-existing apparatus," with "a thing-like quality" (1997, 15). That is, according to Hester and Eglin, Sacks's membership categories and the rules related to them can be seen as machinery in "some pre-given and decontextualized sense" and in a "once-and-for-all manner" (1997, 16). For example, categories from the collections of sex and family appear to be described "out of context" (1997, 15).

Interestingly, this kind of objection was expressed by Lynch and Livingston with regard to the problem of rule governed behavior which we touched upon above in the discussion of social order. In conclusion, instead of reifying membership categories, ethnomethodologists conceive of them as indexical expressions (Hester and Eglin 1997, 18), as used and invoked by members as 'rule-using creatures' (Hester and Eglin 1992, 16), and as being confirmed in their ontological status only moment by moment through members' activities. Therefore, membership categorizations should be dealt with as "locally and temporally contingent" (Hester and Eglin, 1997, 18), and "with no time out" from the *hic et nunc* (Garfinkel, 1996, 11). Consequently, the self and identity, as elements of a "contextually-occasioned categorial order" (the "self-as-categorized") are inherently temporal and contingent (Watson 1998, 218).

Viewed in these terms, there is no stable, core self or identity in ethnomethodology and conversation analysis. Ethnomethodology and conversation analysis suggest that there is no more to self or identity, beyond members' practical activities *in situ*, in the *hic et nunc*. This picture of the ebb and flow of self/identity with every moment appears to be the mysterious fate of human agency (Mehan and Wood 1975, 374). Self and identity are reborn continually until the moment of death. On the question of whether this life without qualities is a torture or a blessing, ethnomethodology remains completely silent.

In conclusion, it is plausible to say that ethnomethodological terms such as improvisation, *ad hoc* practices, and "playing by ear" (Bittner 1967), associated with passing practices, are closely related to modernity. Also, the emphasis on the *hic et nunc*, contingency, temporality, and the art of performance, are all general features of modernity. Within modern society, the essential aspects of behavior are more likely to be approached, not by means of rules or laws, but by creativity *in situ*. With respect to this, one can argue that ethnomethodology's conceptions refer to particularly modern phenomena, although the theme of modernity is never discussed in Garfinkel's works, and although Garfinkel does not intend any reference to modernity.

CONCLUSION

The relationship between modernity and modern sociological theory is a problem that is remarkably neglected, even though it has great bearing upon a range of fundamental theoretical and empirical questions. I have tried to remedy this neglect somewhat by identifying what specifically is modern in the works of three modern sociological theorists, Parsons, Goffman, and Garfinkel. I have focused especially on how their landmark analyses of human agency and social order reflect characteristics of modernity, regardless of whether the theories address modernity explicitly or not.

The analyses above have many interesting and important ramifications, but I would like to single out two for emphasis. First, and most basically, these three bodies of theory can be read as reflecting modern social conditions, and actually open up to such a reading, revealing new dimensions and depth. Second, previous readings and comparisons of these theories can be re-evaluated in light of the above analyses and connections. Viewed as alternate reflections of modern social conditions, the differences between the three bodies of theory become somewhat attenuated. Far from being mutually incommensurable or mutually irrelevant, the three bodies of theory share at least a common ground in modern social conditions, and if one traces the reflections of this ground in the three bodies of theory, one can draw significant connections in a literature marked by invidious distinctions. I will suggest the lines along which such connections could be drawn by way of recapitulating and collecting together some of what I have uncovered and suggested in the previous chapters.

PARSONS, GOFFMAN, AND GARFINKEL AS MODERNISTS

In my attempt to characterize Parsons, Goffman, and Garfinkel as modernists, I began by discussing some of the defining social characteristics of modernity. As opposed to pre-modern societies, in which traditional social patterns were routinely followed and honored, modern society is one of relative irregularity, inconsistency, instability, and unpredictability. The modern world is therefore one of uncertainty, with new troubles and new dangers. Modern society is also a more abstract society, due to processes such as de-institutionalization. Modernity is remarkable, then, for a loss of existential grounding. Similarly, modern society is characterized by a high degree of anonymity, opaqueness, and ambiguity. For many of the same reasons, modernity undercuts uniqueness and personal identity. This occurs largely by means of the standardization and leveling of persons and practices, with a resulting emphasis on function and replaceability. All of these features of modernity proceed exactly in line with the increasing pluralization of society.

In response to these modern conditions, modern man often turns his eyes inward, for example through the process of subjectivization. Modern man can therefore be described as increasingly conscious of self, at the same time that he is increasingly skeptical and alienated in relation to others, even in some senses a stranger in his own society.

The modern subject thus needs to be understood as arising in and struggling with problematic modern social conditions. This is not to say, however, that the modern subject is merely an existential victim. It should be clear that modern social conditions pose modern problems to modern subjects, but they also provide modern subjects with an increasing range of choices, opportunities, and forms of freedom. Modern developments can therefore be met with enthusiasm as well as uncertainty. More importantly, new freedoms can be used to search for new sources of order and authenticity. The same modern social conditions that give rise to uncertainty, anonymity and the like thus give rise to new possibilities and the freedom to pursue them. Modernity must therefore be understood as a constellation of diverse social conditions and processes, with equally diverse and sometimes contradictory consequences for modern subjects.

It is for precisely these reasons that many of the most perceptive modern theorists, as well as the most profound theorists of modernity, display a marked ambivalence in their work. Such ambivalence has often been held against one or another modern theorist, for example, as a symptom of personal confusion or inconsistency, but it now needs to be recognized that modernity is complex and multi-faceted; any insightful analysis, and especially any penetrating evaluation, should recognize and reflect this complexity. It is not a question of personal confusion about an unambiguous phenomenon, but a question of personal insight into a phenomenon which is in many respects ambiguous.

In the case of Parsons, I have analyzed both his explicit writings on modern society and the implicit understanding of modernity that informs his work. With regard to his explicit coverage of modern social conditions, I have considered his conceptions of pluralism, role pluralism, inclusion, adaptive upgrading, the vital center, value generalization, instrumental activism, institutionalized individualism, and diffusely enduring solidarity. In each case, Parsons's concern can be identified as a peculiarly or especially modern concern.

At the level of implicit understanding, I examined Parsons's general theory of action to see whether it reflected especially modern realities. In fact, it reveals a number of modern characteristics, both with respect to social order and with respect to the individual. Despite his aim of demonstrating order, the social order Parsons portrays is, in all truth, a precarious or problematic order. He describes an order characterized by contingency and temporality, inconsistencies, irregularities, and ambiguities, instability, and unpredictability, and related to all of these, the attenuation of consensual values and norms. Individuals are portrayed as both abstract and contingent, persons without qualities, anonymous and free. Following from his understanding of society and his understanding of the individual, Parsons sees the bonds between individuals and society as weak and endangered.

Both in respect to Parsons's explicit theoretical system and with respect to his implicit understanding of modernity, we can draw the conclusion that Parsons sees the social world as an essentially precarious, vulnerable, and fragile one. Parsons's conceptions of social order and human agency thus reflect the characteristics of modern society very well; they are especially sensitive to what I have called the abstraction of society, the mutual autonomization of the institutional order and the individual, the crisis of internalization, and the growth of individualism.

In the case of Goffman, I have focused on his conceptions of ritual order (ritual equilibrium and ritual disequilibrium), interaction order, and frame. With respect to the various orders of social life, Goffman observes that institutional order is minimal in modern society, and that ritual order provides some of the regularity and stability that the institutional order can no longer provide. But then he discloses that the ritual order is itself vague and unstable, and suggests that the interaction order is the most significant in modern society. The interaction order, however, is in turn revealed to be fragile.

Goffman discusses another type of order, cognitive order, in his treatment of frames. But, just as previous types of order were seen to be problematic, frames, too, are revealed to be precarious, finite, and temporary. Individuals are portrayed as confronting ambiguity and uncertainty, and this ambiguity and uncertainty are observed to be increasing in modern society. Such instability and uncertainty, in turn, is suggested to have a clear impact upon individuals, who themselves become unstable and opaque. The individual is portrayed as skeptical and wary, loose in a world of strangers, with little to fall back upon except the skills of impression management and a fragile trust.

Following from these discussions, it is clear that Goffman's views of social order and human agency substantially reflect characteristics of modern society, especially those of pluralism, abstraction, ambiguity, and anonymity. Goffman's views of order and agency are, throughout, the views of a keen observer of modern society.

Finally, I addressed Garfinkel's writings, and ethnomethodology and conversation analysis more generally, as bodies of work which reflect modern social conditions. According to Garfinkel and those who have followed his work, the social world is filled with order, yet this order cannot be captured except as a local achievement of the ordinary practical activities of members. Consequently, social order is envisioned as inherently and extremely contingent and temporal, and, by extension, extremely precarious.

Most importantly, Garfinkel emphasizes that the taken-for-granted social world is replete with, even rooted upon, ambiguity and uncertainty. Garfinkel describes how members actually produce and sustain a sense of stability in the teeth of ambiguity, and out of endemically ambiguous materials. In doing so, Garfinkel emphasizes the 'just thisness' (*haecceities*) of the 'here and now' (*hic et nunc*), and the necessity of improvised (*ad libitum*), artful, *ad hocing* practices in members' attempts to understand the unique, ambiguous details of situated action as exhibiting an underlying intersubjective order. Consequently, Garfinkel's vision sees no core, either to social order or to the self. Both are contingent and temporal. Again, we have a theory of social order and human agency which captures primary characteristics of modern social life.

A BRIEF COMPARISON

If I have been successful in portraying Parsons, Goffman, and Garfinkel as modernists, then one question which follows is how the three theorists compare to each other *qua* modernists. This involves noting similarities and differences which are only apparent after one has attempted to read and compare these theorists in the socio-historical context of modernity.

On the problem of social order, all three theorists refuse to treat order as a *fait accompli*, instead treating it as problematic, contingent, and temporal. In this they are clearly, and similarly, modern. This said, the three theorists also adopt distinctly different strategies for locating this problematic order. Whereas Parsons portrays order at the macro level, as a vague, abstract, and distal wholeness, Goffman studies micro order, in observable social ritual and interaction, and Garfinkel respecifies order of all kinds as locally produced by members *in situ*, in the *hic et nunc* (here and now). The three authors thus share a modern understanding of order, but pursue this order in significantly different directions.

Even in their differences, though, they display similarly modern concerns with phenomena that, retrospectively, are best understood as symptoms of modernity.

On the problems of the individual and human agency, the three theorists also share important similarities. Each portrays the human being as an undetermined, amorphous, ephemeral, anonymous being, continually faced with contingency and uncertainty. Significantly, the three theorists also share an understanding of man as autonomous vis-à-vis rules, norms, and roles. In these respects, each theorist has captured the modern condition in much the same way.

Parsons, Goffman, and Garfinkel differ, however, in what they make of the modern condition. For Parsons, the fact that man has no inherent qualities entails freedom and the possibility for self-development. At least in his general theory of action, freedom is seen as a blessing rather than a source of alienation. In contrast, Goffman seems to regard this boundless freedom as a burden, and seems to give up on the pursuit of self which it allows. He sees in human agency the possibility of transcending this contingent, ephemeral existence in some manner, and begins to explore this possibility. Lastly, Garfinkel is analytically indifferent to such questions. The self and agency as theoretical or general problems are abandoned entirely when members' methods of practical action and practical reasoning are made the exclusive topic of inquiry. One can talk about contingent practices of invoking or describing selves, but 'the self' as an abstract entity dies away. Similarly, agency becomes the occasioned and practical concern of members, rather than a theoretical contention.

As with the problem of social order, the differences between the three approaches to agency and self are very significant, but whether one sees new possibilities for personal development, a new need for transcendence, or a need for human studies to forego such traditional concerns, the sensibility displayed is a decidedly modern sensibility.

NOTES

INTRODUCTION

1. 'Modern sociological theory' is often used interchangeably with 'contemporary sociological theory,' but some classical sociological theory is very modern, and some contemporary theory is not. 'Modern' is here used to characterize content or substance, and 'contemporary' is used to refer to the time period of a work. For my purposes, 'post-modern' sociological theory can be considered a variety of 'modern' sociological theory; any division between 'post-modern' and 'modern' sociological theory would obscure the degree to which 'modern' sociological theory was already concerned with ostensibly 'post-modern' themes.

2. I will offer a more detailed treatment of these themes further on, in chapter 4.

CHAPTER 1. ON MODERNITY

1. I benefit from the new translation of Weber's classic, by Stephen Kalberg (Weber 2001).

2. Cf. Berger, Berger and Kellner (1973).

3. Cf. Giddens (1991, 6). He suggests that modernity procreates "differences, exclusion and marginalisation."

4. Cf. Giddens (1992, 175).

5. Cf. Berger and Neuhaus (1970, 30).

6. Although they themselves make no deliberate, direct efforts to relate their concept of "stranger" to the problem of modernity, Alfred Schutz and Georg Simmel provide us with succinct treatments of the stranger which are relevant for understanding modern man. See Schutz's "The Stranger"(1964b), and Simmel "The Stranger" (1950).

7. "Typification," Schutz notes, "is indeed that form of abstraction which leads to the more or less standardized yet more or less vague, conceptualization of common-sense thinking and to the necessary ambiguity of the terms of the ordinary vernacular" (1962, 323). Natanson, in his *Phenomenology, Role, and Reason*, indicates that, for Schutz, 'typification' can be expressed in manifold ways, such as 'abstraction,' 'anonymity,' and 'transcendence' (1974, 69).

8. De-institutionalization will be discussed below. For a further introduction to and explanation of Gehlen's theory of institutions and its application to the modern situation, see Berger and Kellner's "Arnold Gehlen and the theory of institution" (1965), and *Sociology Reinterpreted* (1981), and Berger's "Foreword" in the English translation of Arnold Gehlen's *Man in the Age of Technology* (1980), and Zijderveld (1979). Gehlen's original work on institutions (*Urmensch und Spätkultur* [1956]) is not available in English yet.

9. With reference to W. I. Thomas, one could say modern man has great difficulty defining his situation.

10. This concept can be understood as abstraction and anonymity in Simmel's work.

11. Benjamin develops this theory in addressing the effect of industrialization on art (1969).

12. On the theory of 'leveling' in modern society, c.f. Ortega y Gasset (1964, 26).

13. We can understand clichés as adapting man to this predicament.

14. The term 'symbolic token' is taken from Giddens (1990, 22).

15. For sociological criticisms of this novel, see Berger (1970a and 1992).

16. Clichés are thus similar to laughter, since both contribute primarily to a kind of relief (Zijderveld 1979, 60; Berger 1997).

17. Cf. Calinescu (1987, 48–50).

18. C.f. one of the most famous phrases in Marx and Engels' *Communist Manifesto*:

> All fixed, fast-frozen relations, with their train of ancient and venerable prejudices and opinions are swept away, all new-formed ones become antiquated before they can ossify. All that is solid melts into air, all that is holy is profaned, and man is at last compelled to face with sober senses, his real conditions of life, and his relations with his kind. (Marx and Engels 1967, 83)

19. Consider the relative ease with which modern man seems to dispose of friends, even spouses.

20. Cf. Giddens (1991, 33).

21. Cf. Musil's novel, *The Man Without Qualities* (1996).

22. Cf. Kellner (1992, 141–2).

23. Cf. Frisby (1986).

24. The problem of 'ennui' has been one of the major subjects in modern existential writing. See also, Kellner (1992, 142).

25. See Zijderveld (1979, 35).

26. Cf. Kolb (1986).

27. Cf. Otto Rank (1971). According to Rank, with the process of modernization, including the growing abstraction and the reality-loss of the institutional order, "the otherness," which was previously located outside of human beings, becomes internalized. Rank identifies this as a theme in modern literature. Weber also emphasizes the importance of the private realm in modernity: "Precisely the ultimate and most sublime values have retreated from public life either into the transcendental realm of mystic life or into the brotherliness of direct and personal human relations" (1946, 155). For a further discussion of the emergence of 'subjectivization,' see Horowitz and Maley (1994), Dallmayr (1994), Maley (1994), and Horowitz (1994). See also, Hannah Arendt (1998, 69).

28. For a general discussion of modern man's attempts to escape from the press of everyday life, including his social roles, see Cohen and Taylor's *Escape Attempts* (1992).

29. Berger (1961; also cf. 1963).

30. In his article "Sincerity and Authenticity" (1973), Berger suggests that authenticity implies a "fundamental opposition" between self

and society; by contrast, sincerity exhibits a "symmetrical relation" between them.

31. Weber (1946; 1963). This is often described as 'secularization.' Despite recent counter-secularizing movements around the world, there can be no doubt that the once formidable influence of religion has been significantly weakened.

32. Berger argues that "bad faith is the denial of freedom" (1961, 94).

33. See Lionel Trilling's *Sincerity and Authenticity* (1972).

34. In his *The Journeying Self*, Natanson writes that "to speak of Bad Faith may appear paradoxical, but nevertheless it is essential to understand that the self which has become routinized in its role activity is not a 'bad' self but merely one which articulates its experience in a certain way" (1970a, 45).

35. Natanson succinctly notes that "along with the dangers of anonymizations, there are also remarkable possibilities, a freedom which roles and role-taking make possible" (1970, 45–6). Unfortunately, so far in the contemporary social sciences, if one wants to emphasize freedom with regard to roles, he tends to speak only of the term 'role-making,' as a brilliant device invented for explaining freedom, ignoring the possibility of freedom or transcendence in role-taking. For a further explanation of the concept of 'role-making,' see Ralph Turner (1955–56; 1962).

36. The term 'transcendence' is not used in any esoteric philosophical sense. To transcend means simply to go beyond. For a similar account of transcendence, see Natanson (1974, 75). Transcendence can therefore be understood as a kind of freedom.

37. Cf. Giddens (1990, 145).

38. The origin of the existential suffering of man can be seen in the fact that man is a "deficient being *(Maengelwesen)*" (Gehlen 1988, 13). That is, compared with animals, human beings are characterized by a "lack of instinct."

39. See Gehlen's discussion of 'primitivism' in his *Man in the Age of Technology* (1980, 43).

40. Eccentricity, in philosophical anthropology, can be understood as a drive to go beyond the here and now.

41. Cf. Helmut Schelsky (1987, 135). Here he suggests that "eccentricity has grown and been transformed" rapidly and remarkably in modern society.

42. Cf. Giddens (1990, 14). And see also Meyrowitz's *No Sense of Place* (1985). He claims that the modern electronic media have severely undermined modern man's distinctive sense of place.

43. Cf. Giddens (1991). According to Giddens, the *Umwelt* "includes awareness of high consequence of risks, which represent dangers from which no one can get completely out range" (1991, 128).

44. The metaphor of the 'cave' is drawn from Marx (1978), Simone Weil (1963), and Berger (1961). Weil cogently notes: "Society is the cave. The way out is solitude" (145). The cave can also be understood as a "symbolic universe," in Berger's terms (1967, 1974). Zenkins uses the term "umbrella" in a similar context. (1996, 123). See also Giddens's term "protective cocoon" (1991).

CHAPTER 2. TALCOTT PARSONS

1. For an example of the attempt to interpret Parsons's theory in the Kantian tradition, see Münch (1981; 1982).

2. Cf. Hamilton (1983, 67); Bourricaud (1981, 3); Lidz (1991a).

3. As Parsons notes, "every system, including both its theoretical propositions and its main relevant empirical insights, may be visualized as an illuminated spot enveloped by darkness" (1937, 17).

4. For a detailed discussion of Parsons's analytical realism, see Hamilton (1983, 64–5).

5. Cf. Bourricaud (1981, 27).

6. Parsons' defines the collection of pattern variables as "a conceptual scheme for classifying the components of an action system" (1967, 194). Some of the germinal dichotomies of the pattern variables are laid out in Parsons's paper "Propaganda and Social Control" (1942), which later appeared in his *Essays in Sociological Theory* (1954). They are fully developed in Parsons and Shils's *Toward a General Theory of Action* (1951). However, among the dichotomies of the pattern variables, "ascription/achievement" was replaced by "quality/performance" in Parsons' later paper, "Pattern Variables Revisited: A Response to Dubin" (1967 [1960]).

7. Parsons (1951, 4) and Parsons et al. (1953, 140–3).

8. For a detailed elaboration of reductionism, see Bourricaud (1981, 55).

9. Within this context, Parsons cautiously speaks of the "atemporal" world of meaning (1937, 636, 763). It should be noted, however, that the world of meaning is only meant to be "atemporal" relative to action at a specific time. He does not mean that cultural systems last forever.

10. In other words, norms can be "legitimated by values, but not vice versa" (Parsons 1967, 10).

11. According to Bourricaud, Parsons acknowledges or even emphasizes the distinctions between norms and laws of nature, reacting against Durkheim's positivism. That is, norms (moral and even legal obligations) are "not constraining in the same way as the laws of gravity" (Bourricaud 1981, 153). "No normative system," as Bourricaud points out, is "inherently effective, certainly not unaided" (1981, 152).

12. Instead of the term internalization, Parsons often uses the term "introjection." Both are borrowed from Freud. See, Parsons (1977, 37).

13. Bourricaud argues that the notion of socialization in Parsons's theory implies "a degree of plasticity" in actors, "some responsiveness" in actors, and "the possibility of success or failure" (1981, 48).

14. This famous AGIL four function paradigm is fully developed in Parsons, Bales, and Shils's *Working Papers in the Theory of Action* (1953).

15. Social control is defined by Parsons as "processes in the social system which tend to counteract the deviant tendencies" (1951, 297).

16. See Jonathan Turner and Leonard Beeghley (1974), Turner (1974), and Scott (1974). Turner and Beeghley insist that the voluntaristic theory of action has been the most important feature of Parsons's intellectual work and serves as a cornerstone for his whole corpus. Although the voluntaristic aspects of Parsons's theory are often unrecognized, theorists like Scott (1974) and Gould (1989) try to correct this misunderstanding.

17. Cf. Black (1961); Walsh (1972); Giddens (1979); Mouzelis (1995). Walsh states that concrete human individuals have been excluded from the social system (1972, 61). Giddens, summarizing criticisms of Parsons's view of man, argues that "human agents seem to elude the grasp of his scheme: the stage is set, the scripts written, the roles established, but the performers are curiously absent from the scene" (1979, 253). And, Mouzelis notes that in Parsons' sociology actors are endlessly rehearsing their roles without ever acting" (1995, 77).

18. The term *Homo parsoniensis* was coined by Bourricaud (1981, 100), to establish a new interpretation of the Parsonian view of man against the existing view of critics.

19. Dennis H. Wrong's famous article (1961) would be a representative of this claim.

20. Of course, interpretations of Parsons's voluntarism vary. For a further discussion of Parsons' voluntarism, see, e.g., Alexander (1983; 1987; 1988), Barnes (1981), Bourricaud (1981), Fitzhenry (1986b), Gould (1989; 1991), Hamilton (1983), Holton and Turner (1986b), Lemert (1979), and Robertson and Turner (1991). See also Parsons's article replying to Wrong (1962). Parsons argues that the individual has to be viewed in terms of 'institutionalized individualism.' For a detailed explanation of institutionalized individualism and an extended application of this concept to modern society, see Parsons (1977, 168).

21. Cf. Alexander (1978; 1987a, 28; 1988, 98).

22. For a further discussion of the limits of Alexander's interpretation of Parsons's voluntarism, see Gould (1991). Gould also criticizes Camic's (1989, 90–1) and Alexander's (1983, 35) definitions of voluntarism as freedom vis-à-vis the conditions of action.

23. For example, see Holton and Turner (1986a; 1986b), Lechner (1991), and Robertson and Turner (1991).

24. In fact, Parsons writes a 16-page section draft on Simmel for inclusion in his *The Structure of Social Action* (1937), though he later withdraws it from the final draft. (Alexander 1987b, 38; Levine 1991, 188). See also Parsons ([1935] 1991, 231–57; 1977, 165; 1979, 2).

25. Cf. Garfinkel's unpublished book, *Parsons Primer* (1960), in which he notes that "for Parsons the study of social organizations of concerted action consists of the study of the ways in which the social structures which consists of numbers of sociologically typified persons in sociologically typified territories with typified distributions and typified relationships between them all governed by typified rules are so conceived as to attend their related character" (1960, 64).

26. It is very surprising that phenomenological insights can provide a plausible answer to this tricky question, given that the Parsons-Schutz debate has been characterized as a "dialogue of the deaf" (Coser 1979, 680). On the debate between these leading contemporary sociologists, see Grathoff's *The Theory of Social Action: The Correspondence of Alfred Schutz and Talcott Parsons* (1978). For a critical review of this book, see Giddens (1983, 76–81). And, on the possibility of a convergence between Parsonian and phenomenological theory, see Jules-Rosette (1980). Also, on the possibility of new synthesis between Parsons's theory and competing theories, see Münch (1987).

27. As I will show later, this argument only applies to Parsons's action theory (or general theory of action). He explicitly acknowledges the other side of anonymity, i.e., alienation, in his theory of change.

28. In this regard, Lemert argues that Parsons's theory of action represents typical "homocentrism" (1979).

29. Cf. Bourricaud (1981, 294).

30. Cf. Bourricaud (1981, 101).

31. Dennis Wrong, despite his early famous criticism of Parsons, later views Parsons as a post-Wittgensteinian analytic philosopher of action. See his recent work *The Problem of Order* (1994, 105).

32. Parsons puts it this way: "the problem of stability introduces considerations of temporal continuity" (1961, 41).

33. Again, Parsons discusses alienation in modern society when he addresses social change.

34. See, e.g., Parsons (1967, 8–9; 1964, 28) for illustrations re. sex roles.

35. For a critique of this position, see Hans Joas (1993). He argues that the concept of "role distance" (coined and elaborated by Erving Goffman) is not observable in Parsons's theory, because Parsons assumes "unconscious" conformity with role expectations "as a result of actors' prior internalization of the associated value orientation" (1993, 222). Based upon my reading of Parsons, I think this critique is extremely misleading.

36. Wrong's argument that Parsons has neither a theory of human nature, nor a general conception of man, is quite valid (Wrong 1994, 108).

37. Bourricaud (1981, 261). Cf. Parsons (1977, 172), where Parsons argues that "as with the personality and social system, there can be no one-to-one correspondence between the properties of an organism and the personality's internalized content of normative culture, and social role expectations."

38. Inclusion is defined as "the process by which previously excluded groups attain full citizenship or membership in the societal community" (Parsons 1967, 428–9).

39. Parsons (1964, 196, 277, 278; 1977, 303; 1978, 279).

40. See Parsons and Platt (1973, 42), and Parsons (1977, 168, 308).

41. Schneider, *American Kinship* in Parsons (1977, 390).

42. Cf. Holton and Turner (1986b, 231).

43. For Parsons, the empirical world is conceived as "disorder" or "chaos" (Hamilton 1983, 67). Cf. Robertson and Turner, who claim that "Parsons's interest in the analytical aspects of order pivoted upon his acute sensitivity to empirical disorder" (1991, 13).

44. Parsons notes that "the breakdown of any given normative order, that is a state of chaos from a normative point of view, may well result in an order in the factual sense, that is a state of affairs susceptible of scientific analysis" (1937, 91–2).

45. Cf. Holton and Turner (1986a; 1986b).

46. Lechner (1991, 184). It should be clearly noted that this wholeness is quite different from "the world's oneness" (Gouldner 1970, 209), which characterizes political movements like Nazism and Fascism. Parsons vehemently and aggressively rejects these movements or ideologies. Parsons conceives of fascism as a distorted reaction to modern society and an attempt to return to *Gemeinschaft*. It means a restriction and suppression of the autonomy of human beings, and is therefore unbearable for Parsons. In contrast to "the world's oneness," Parsons's wholeness is a ground for the autonomy of the individual; it is not constraining, but a feeble, vague, abstract, even empty symbol or image. For the refutation of Gouldner's critique of Parsons, see Lemert (1979, 97). And, for a detailed discussion of Parsons's objection to the Fascist Nazi movement, see Parsons (1969).

47. For a representative example of this argument, see Walsh (1972, 61).

CHAPTER 3. ERVING GOFFMAN

1. The difference between Gouldner's and Giddens's appraisals are an interesting example. Gouldner, in his *The Coming Crisis of Western Sociology* (1970), argues that Goffman advocates the ideology of the middle class bourgeoisie who are retreating from the serious matters of the world, like economic inequality, into snobbish aesthetics. Put differently, Gouldner claims that the world Goffman describes reflects nothing but a specific class in advanced capitalist Western society (1970, 379–81). By contrast, Giddens says that Goffman's approach allows a much wider analysis, even though Goffman's studies dealt almost exclusively with

Western civil society. That is, Goffman's work can be seen to identify "novel characteristics of the contemporary era" and to hold up "a mirror to many worlds, not just to one" (Giddens 1984, 70).

2. But, to mention some of them in passing, they range from structuralist (Gonos 1977; 1980), Durkheimian (Collins 1980; 1988a; 1988b; 1994), and unshakably empiricist (Burns 1992, 23), to situationalist and individualist (Knorr-Cetina 1981; Campbell 1996, 45), symbolic interactionist (Fontana 1980), existentialist (Lofland 1980), semiotic (MacCannell 1983), and post-modernist *avant la lettre* (Clough 1990; Battershill 1990).

3. Among those who interpret Goffman in this way are Gouldner (1970, 378–90), MacIntyre (1969, 447–8; 1981, 30–1, 109, 115–17), Brittan (1977, 112), Habermas (1984, 90–4), and Hollis (1985, 226). These criticisms bemoan the lack of morality in Goffman's understanding of man. These criticisms are directed at Goffman's use of metaphors and analogies such as his dramaturgical metaphor and game analogy. For further methodological criticisms, see Sennett (1977, 36), Ryan (1978, 68), Geertz (1983), Giddens (1984), and Miller (1984).

4. There are multiple opinions on Goffman's characterizations of morality as well. For example, Friedson (1983) describes Goffman as an inveterate moralist because he believes that Goffman is a "celebrant and defender of the self against society" (1983, 361). Others point to Goffman's emphasis on 'trust' (Giddens 1987, 113; Philip Manning 1992, 58), or 'ritual' (Collins 1988; 44). But all of them share the position that the world of interaction Goffman explores is not merely a technical one, but a moral one (cf. Drew and Wooton 1988, 6; Williams 1988).

5. See, e.g., Creelan (1984).

6. I will spell this out in some detail later, but for the moment, I should say that Goffman was never so naïve as to confuse rituals with the sacred.

7. Here, I include works ranging from Goffman's pre-doctoral writings to some articles which are reprinted in his 1967 collection, *Interaction Ritual*. Even though *The Presentation of Self in Everyday Life* was published in 1956, I place it in the second stage.

8. In addition to ceremonial rules, Goffman refers to "substantive rules" (1967, 53) as a counterpart to ceremonial rules. He also mentions another dimension of rules by distinguishing symmetrical from asymmetrical rules (1967, 52–53). However, as Goffman himself confesses,

his overriding concern is with ceremonial rules, and indeed, he restricts his attention to them (Goffman 1967, 55).

9. Ritual equilibrium arises from the result of the "face-work" (Goffman 1967, 12) of "self-regulating participants in social encounters" (Goffman 1967, 44).

10. Cf. Creelan (1984, 673).

11. In this stage, I include most of his work, ranging from his late 1950s work, *The Presentation of Self in Everyday Life* (1959), to his 1980s work. However, I exclude his *Frame Analysis* (1974) from this stage, putting it in his last stage.

12. Lemert argues that Goffman's version of social life is filled with strategic and dark secrets (1995, 194).

13. In Goffman's terms, the 'substantive rule' (1967, 53) and 'substantive norms' lose considerable significance for the practical conduct of individuals in modern times (1971, 96).

14. Goffman (1971, 96). Even though Goffman mentions several kinds of norms, he seems to focus on "ritual norms," which regulate "displays, ceremonies, expressions, and other bits of conduct whose primary significance lies in the attitude which the actor can therewith take up to objects of ultimate value" (Goffman 1971, 96).

15. Creelan, while claiming that the chronological sequence of Goffman's work follows the sequence of events and issues in Job, argues that Goffman portrays the individual along the lines of those who act as if they are guardians of all kinds of moral and ritual code, exactly like Job's three friends, Eliphaz, Bildad and Zophar, who came to Job to console him. That is, they are portrayed "as impious and hypocritical power-seekers, whose attachment to the conventional theology and its ritual code is simultaneously their totally idolatrous preoccupation with their own wealth and power" (Creelan 1984, 680).

16. For the definition of 'total institution,' see Goffman (1961a, xiii).

17. Obviously, the best example of the kind of cooperation at issue now is the "institutional display" involved in an open house at a mental hospital, involving the cooperation between staff and inmates (Goffman 1961a, 101).

18. Cf. Fontana (1980). Fontana paraphrases Goffman's portraits of modern life in this way: "we are but wild beasts in a jungle, ready to spring at all times. Interaction has become very thin ice in a society in

which safe presentations may hide danger. The ice is thin and may break at any time, but, doomed to our way of life, we go on skating" (1980, 73).

19. Goffman quotes from Edward Ross's *Social Control* (1908) in order to develop his notion of this type of order: "But when all who meet or overtake one another in crowded ways take the time and pains needed to avoid collision, the throng is orderly. Now, at the bottom of the notion of social order lies the same idea" (Ross 1908, 1; quoted in Goffman 1971, 6).

20. In Goffman's terms, 'externalization' (or 'body gloss,') and 'scanning,' are considered the "two processes important in the organization of public life" when people walk and pass each other. See Goffman (1971, 11).

21. Goffman speaks of the "immediate presence of others" (1983b, 2) and "co-bodily presence" (1983b, 4). For this reason, Giddens (1984) calls Goffman a theorist of co-presence.

22. Using the traffic analogy, the interaction order exists even without any help from traffic signs, road signs, or police, and needless to say, without traffic laws.

23. For a description of the weakness of the institutional order, see Goffman's example of the modern nation state. He suggests: "To be sure, the interaction order prevailing even in the most public places is not a creation of the apparatus of a state. Certainly most of this order comes into being and is sustained from below as it were, in some cases in spite of overarching authority not because of it" (Goffman 1983b, 6).

24. To that extent, rules governing service transactions might remind one of the "fundamental democracy" which Goffman mentioned earlier in his *Presentation of Self in Everyday Life* (1959, 235).

25. Goffman elsewhere refers to them as "realms of being" (1974, 563). Cf. Burns (1992, 239).

26. Goffman also uses the term "organization," instead of the term, "structure" (1974, 11).

27. Cf. Rawls (1983; 1987; 1989b). Rawls distinguishes two categories of order in Goffman's work: constitutive order and framing order. However, my reading suggests that Goffman never uses the term 'framing order,' instead, but rather, "framing process" (1974, 439), and only when the notion of frame is extended to the terrain of activity beyond the purely cognitive arena of frames.

28. 'Keying' refers to the use of a key, a "set of conventions by which a given activity, one already meaningful in terms of some primary framework, is transformed into something patterned on this activity but seen by the participants to be something quite else." And, he goes on to state that "the process of transcription can be called keying" (Goffman 1974, 43–44). Some basic keys employed in our society, Goffman suggests, are "make-believe" (e.g., playfulness, fantasy or daydreaming, and dramatic scriptings), "contests," "ceremonials," "technical redoing" (e.g., practicings, demonstrations, replicative records of events, group psychotherapy and other role playing sessions, and experiments), and "regroundings" (1974, 48–77).

29. See the chapter on "Designs and Fabrication" in Goffman's *Frame Analysis*.

30. It is hardly possible for modern society to anchor the individual through roles, because of role distance. Resource continuity also seems to be severely undermined, because uniqueness and style, which are representative examples of continuity, have disappeared (1974, 289). Unconnectedness rarely occurs, because most people are likely to compare and contrast different frames and activities, thus raising doubts and questions. Among the anchoring devices, only the "human being" seems not to be disturbed in modern society. Rather, the "human being" device appears to become reinforced. However, the concept of human being itself is a quite ambiguous one. It is not sufficient, by itself, to anchor the individual in the world. Even though "human being" is a prominent anchoring device, it does not anchor activity very well, especially compared to the anchoring made possible by unquestioning identification with a role, such as 'farmer,' which was characteristic in pre-modern times.

31. As Goffman points out, ambiguity, misframings and frame disputes are different constitutive elements in framing (1974, 324).

32. For an example of this type of frame-breaking, we shall refer to the following striking story provided by Goffman:

> The [Bach Aria] Group, which includes [tenor Jan] Peerce, Soprano Eileen Farrell, two other fine singers and a chamber group, gives sedate, even austere recitals—everybody dressed in black, sitting primly in straight-backed chairs onstage and being very, very dignified, as befits Bach.

> Before one recital Peerce was backstage warming up his remarkable vocal cords and hitting one high C after another, as Miss Farrell listened in wonderment. At last she asked, "How

do you do it, Jan? How do you hit those high ones so effort-
lessly?" "Easy, Eileen," he smiled. "I just imagine I'm being
goosed by an ice-cream cone."

A few minutes later the Bach Aria Group filed onstage—
serious and proper—and took its seats. As Peerce started to
arise for his first solo, Miss Farrell whispered something,
whereupon he fell back, helplessly convulsed with laughter; in
this instance the show did NOT go on and the delicate mood
was never restored. What she had whispered was: "What
flavor?" (Goffman 1974, 351; this story originally appeared in
the *San Francisco Chronicle*, Nov. 8, 1964)

33. In Goffman's terms, "boredom" and "engrossment" (1974, 378).

34. Cf. Simmel (1978).

35. Of course, Goffman also warns of an oversimplification or
overgeneralization of the argument. He states that "the vulnerabilities of
the organization of our experience are not necessarily the vulnerability of
our life in society" (Goffman 1974, 439).

36. Lawrence M. Friedman, "The Law of the Living, the Law of the
Dead: Property, Succession, and Society," *Wisconsin Law Review*, CCCXL
(1966, 373–74; quoted by Goffman 1974, 354).

37. Goffman devotes some time to laughter in *Frame Analysis*, and
associates it with Henri Bergson's insights on laughter. Goffman sees
laughter as significant in explaining the possibility of breaking frame, but
he is also aware of the nature of laughter, which implies the intrinsic
possibility of transcendence; laughter is like lava coming out of the vol-
cano of the discrepancy between frames. One can also mention Peter
Berger's latest work, *Redeeming Laughter* (1997). It is very interesting
that two leading sociologists of the contemporary era show a common
interest in laugher.

38. It is worthwhile quoting Goffman's formulation of the 'negative
experience.' He states:

> When, for whatever reason, the individual breaks frame and
> perceives he has done so, the nature of his engrossment and
> belief suddenly changes. Such reservations as he had about the
> ongoing activity are suddenly disrupted, and, momentarily at
> least, he is likely to become intensively involved with his
> predicament. . . . He is thrust immediately into his predicament
> without the usual defenses. (Goffman 1974, 378–79)

39. Moreover, Goffman points out the possibility of dramatic change for the individual in this respect. He provides:

> Something more than the capsizing of an individual can be involved in frame breaking. If the whole frame can be shaken, rendered problematic, then this, too, can ensure that prior involvements—and prior distances—can be broken up and that, whatever else happens, a dramatic change can occur in what it is that is being experienced. What then *is* experienced is hard, of course, to specify in a positive way; but it can be said what isn't experienced, namely, easy acceptance of the prior conception of what was going on. So one deals again with negative experiences. (Goffman 1974, 382)

40. At this moment, one might remember the term *imago mundi* which is used by Mircea Eliade. In his famous book *The Sacred and the Profane* (1959, 42), Eliade uses this term in order to indicate the fact that humanly created things can present an image (or imitation) of the universe (or the heavens).

41. Creelan's interpretation of the mystery of the frame explored by Goffman is indicated in the following: "While these paradigmatic 'frames' are always provisionally constructed, ever imperfect, symbols of a people's aspiration toward what transcends them, they nevertheless hold a positive, though limited, meaning in this symbolic function" (Creelan 1984, 672).

While arguing that the image of the frame is derived from the Bible, i.e., from the Ark of the Covenant as a wooden frame structure with many layers of gold upon it, Creelan points out the blasphemous possibility of "a form of idolatry" of the Ark [frame] itself, but, at the same time, points out the possibility that it is significant "as a means of representing the ineffable world and Presence of God, whose utterances on a given occasion could not be predicted in advance" (Creelan 1984, 688–92).

42. To that extent, Rawls's observation that for Goffman "playing your role is a moral commitment" (1989, 156) is quite plausible. Nevertheless, I disagree with her on another point; Goffman suggests the possibility of authentic involvement with the infinite transcendent Sacred, not with the institutional order, as Rawls suggest.

43. Cf. Creelan (1984, 687).

44. Creelan (1984, 694).

45. Cf. Burns (1992, 109), Friedson (1983), Verhoeven (1985), Giddens (1987), and Kendon (1988).

46. Goffman states that "the person in our urban secular world is allotted a kind of sacredness that is displayed and confirmed by symbolic acts" (1967, 47). The attribution of sacredness to the self corresponds to Gehlen's concept of 'subjectivization.'

47. Collins (1988b; 1994) points out that Goffman is here indebted to Durkheim's understanding of the modern world. Collins notes that "the self in Goffman is not something that individuals negotiate out of social interaction; it is, rather, the archetypal modern myth. We are compelled to have an individual self, not because we actually have one but because social interaction requires us to act as if we do" (1988b, 50). For a similar argument, see Manning (1992, 60).

48. Collins also indicates that for Goffman, "in modern society . . . rituals center especially around the worship of the self" (1988b, 48).

49. See, e.g., Goffman's example of the freedom with which musicians in an orchestra pit play their roles (1961, 187–88).

50. Goffman (1959, 225; 1967, 59; 1971, 7).

51. One might mention here the preponderant tendency to quest for the authentic self in modern times.

52. To that extent, Collins is quite right when he observes that in Goffman's theory, "the search for the 'ultimate self' will never come to an end" in the human world (Collins 1988b, 63). Also, Schegloff calls this aspect of Goffman work "analytic nihilism," and he goes on to argue that Goffman's analytic nihilism is "motivated by an assertion of human freedom" (Schegloff 1988, 117).

53. Cf. MacCannell (1990, 27). He considers Goffman as one of the first "to describe social life as it is lived as marked by ambiguity and uncertainty, fragmentation, etc."

54. Cf. George Psathas (1977). While describing Goffman's man as a solitary man, he states:

> Man is alone, however. There are no institutions, groups, or organizations which are trying to aid his cause. He struggles alone. He must protect himself. He never organizes others. . . . Goffman's man is paranoid. . . . Goffman leaves man alone, unprotected by friends, relatives, communal associations or institutions. . . . he can only protect himself and himself alone. He does not rally around others or join with them to provide a collective or communal defense. He is alone, thrown into his society alone, and forever to remain alone. (1977, 5–10)

CHAPTER 4. HAROLD GARFINKEL

1. For general discussions of ethnomethodology, see Benson and Hughes (1983), Clayman and Maynard (1995), Heritage (1984; 1987), Livingston (1987), Lynch (1993), Maynard and Clayman (1991), Psathas (1995b; 1989; 1977a; 1994), Sharrock and Anderson (1986), and Wilson and Zimmerman (1980).

2. For extended discussions of conversational analysis, see Clayman and Maynard (1995), Heritage (1984), Lee (1987), and Psathas (1995a).

3. Briefly, ethnomethodology is interested in finding out particulars, rather than theorizing. For further discussions of the ethnomethodological rejection of theorizing, see Lynch (1997; 2001), and Rawls (2000).

4. Cf. Garfinkel's references to 'professional sociology' (Garfinkel and Wieder 1992, 177), formal analysis (Garfinkel 1996, 5; 2001), and the "worldwide social science movement" (Garfinkel 1996, 5).

5. In their paper "On Formal Structures of Practical Actions" (1970), Garfinkel and Sacks mention Wittgenstein's "indicator terms" and their own "indexical expressions." Because ordinary language is often filled with indicator terms, the referential meaning of which is vague and flexible, logicians (especially in the philosophy of language) tried to remedy ordinary language by transforming vague indicator terms into technical or analytical terms, in other words, formulations, which are believed to more accurately and precisely grasp their referential meaning. The concepts of 'indicator term' and 'indexical expression' are central to the arguments against such 'remedies.' For further discussion of Wittgenstein's argument as this relates to ethnomethodology and conversation analysis, see Harvey Sacks's, "Omnirelevant Devices: Settinged Activities, Indicator Terms" (transcribed lecture, February 16, 1967, in *Lectures on Conversation*, Vol. 1. 1992, 512–22) and the first chapter of Lynch's *Scientific Practice and Ordinary Action* (1993).

6. The following excerpt of dialogue illustrates the actual work of formulation:

> Mr. Nields: Did you suggest to the Attorney General that maybe the diversion memorandum and the fact that there was a diversion need not ever come out?
>
> Lt. Col. North: Again, I don't recall that specific conversation at all, but I'm not saying it didn't happen.
>
> Mr. Nields: You don't deny it?

Lt. Col. North: No.

Mr. Nields: You don't deny suggesting to the Attorney General of the United States that he just figure out a way of keeping this diversion document secret?

Lt. Col. North: I don't deny that I said it. I'm not saying I remember it either. (From *Taking the Stand: The Testimony of Lieutenant Colonel Oliver L. North*. New York: Pocket Books, 1987. Quoted in Lynch 1993, 185–86)

7. See, for example, Garfinkel and Sacks's observations that, *a fortiori*: "There is no room in the world *definitively* to propose formulations of activities, identifications, and context" (1970, 359; emphasis added).

8. This position is very similar to that of "ethnomethodological indifference." See Garfinkel and Sacks (1970, 345–46).

9. See also, Garfinkel (2001, 16). C.f. Psathas (1977a, 78; 1980b, 6; 1994, 1162).

10. Garfinkel (1959, 54; 1967a, 36; cf. 1963, 216).

11. Cf. Garfinkel (1996, 8).

12. In a similar vein, Garfinkel suggests the terms 'the missing what' (Garfinkel and Wieder 1992, 203) and "gap" (Garfinkel 1977; Garfinkel, Lynch, and Livingston 1981, 133) for suggesting the blind spot of formal analysis. For example, Garfinkel, Lynch, and Livingston note "the existence of a gap in [the literature of studies of science]: Studies *about* discovering scientists' work are commonplace; Studies *of* their work are rare" (1981, 133).

From the perspective of Garfinkel's ethnomethodology, for example, Howard Becker's (1963) study of dance band musicians talks about, and provides for an exotic and interesting story of, "the culture of jazz musicians," though he never examines "how they manage to play music together" (Lynch 1993, 271). Put differently, "the interactional and improvisational 'work' of playing together—a social phenomenon in its own right" is never discussed by Becker (Lynch 1993, 271).

13. For a further discussion of this term, see Garfinkel and Wieder (1992).

14. As George Psathas says, "order is everywhere" [personal communication.]

15. In his earlier work, Garfinkel describes structure as the "persistence and continuity of the features of concerted action" (1963, 187). Cf. Psathas (1995a, 2; 1990, 17; 1979, 2).

16. It should be noted here that Garfinkel's conceptualization of structure does not deny the existence of macro structures. Rather, for Garfinkel, the ubiquitous repetitiousness and regularity of practical ordinary activities, micro or macro, count as structural phenomena (1996, 7). To that extent, it is severely misleading to claim that ethnomethodology and conversation analysis attend to the micro level. For discussions of this issue, see Coulter (2001, 32) and Rawls (2000, 56).

17. On the same page of his article (1996, 7), Garfinkel adds that "structures are extensively discussed in "Seven Cases with which to Specify How Phenomenal Fields of Ordinary Activities are Lost with Engineering Details of Recording Machinery: Rhythmic Clapping, Summoning Phones, Counting Turns at Talk, Scrubbing the Sink and Other Trivial, Unavoidably Sight-Specific Ordinary Jobs around the House, Traffic Flow, Service Lines, and Computer Supported Real Time Occupations" (1996, 7).

18. Garfinkel (1988, 103, 1001, 18; 1996, 11; Garfinkel and Wieder 1992, 101–103). We will not adopt this convention below, but will occasionally refer to it by the use of 'order' and 'order''.

19. Barry Barnes's (1995) discussion of social order is very suggestive here. He distinguishes three different types of order: First, order as peace, harmony or absence of conflict; second, order as institutional stability, as the persistence or relatively slow change of a given pattern over time; finally, order as pattern. According to Barnes, the first and second types of order are seen as optional, or extras. The third type of order, however, as pattern in human social life, is "evidently not an optional extra" (1995, 12). He characterizes the third type of order as follows: "Always and everywhere, human beings, in peace and war, co-operation and conflict, relate to each other in systematically patterned ways. Always and everywhere, the relations between human beings are linguistically and cognitively, culturally and practically ordered" (Barnes 1995, 17).

20. See also, Clayman and Maynard (1995, 2).

21. Recently, Garfinkel has begun to use the term "autochthonous" as well. See Garfinkel (2001, 15).

22. See also, Sharrock and Button (1991, 141).

23. Cf. Maynard and Wilson (1980).

24. Notice, however, that the term "corpus" was already used by Garfinkel before Zimmerman and Pollner. In his article "Aspects of the Problem of Common-Sense Knowledge of Social Structures" (1959), Garfinkel states that he takes the term "corpus" from Felix Kaufmann.

25. See the following papers of the late Harvey Sacks: "An Initial Investigation of the Usability of Conversational Data for Doing Sociology" (1972), "On the Analyzability of Stories by Children" (1974), "Hotrodder: A Revolutionary Category" (1979), his co-authored paper with E. A. Schegloff "Two Preferences in the Organization of Reference to Persons in Conversation and their Interaction" (Sacks and Schegloff 1979), and his posthumous book, *Lectures on Conversation*, Vol. I: Parts 3 and 5. For recent studies which employ and extend Sacks's membership categorization practices to address the macro issue, see Jayyusi (1984) and Hester and Eglin (1992; 1997).

26. Cf. Sharrock and Watson (1988). For them, social structure might be seen as "incarnate" in social interaction. For Hopper (1991), also, social structure is something humans 'do'.

27. Similarly, Thomas Wilson (1991) suggests: "Social structure consists of matters that are described and oriented to by members of society on relevant occasions as essential resources for conducting their affairs and, at the same time, reproduced as external and constraining social facts through that same social interaction. . . . Social structure is a members' notion, something oriented to by members of society" (1991, 27).

28. Cf. Garfinkel's phrase, "the sense of described social structure" (1959, 54), and Aaron Cicourel's phrase "the sense of social structure" (1976, 328).

29. Cf. Rawls (1989b, 164).

30. Cf. Coulter (1991a, 35).

31. Cf. Heritage (1984, 36).

32. Cf. Rawls (1989b, 165).

33. Cf. Lynch (1993, 22).

34. In his Ph.D. dissertation, written under the guidance of Talcott Parsons, Garfinkel remarks: ". . . the communicator, in organizing the designata, style, and temporal ordering of the signals he generates, in effect leads the person who receives these signals, through the acceptance of meanings to an end state of action whether that end be the purchase of a commodity or an acknowledgement that the communication has been understood." (1952, 368)

35. One of the significant examples of this tendency may be the "documentary method," which members use in their ordinary lives. For a detailed explication of this, see Garfinkel (1967a).

36. In his *Lectures on Conversation*, Sacks claims that the maximization of ambiguity (i.e., indexicality) vis-à-vis ordinary conversational expressions may be the key to the problem of social order (1992, Vol., 1, Lecture 11, 1967).

37. In the Purdue Symposium, Garfinkel provides the panel with an example:

> You can start with a command or you can start with an instruction. "Take a game, any game, write down the instructions as to how to play that game: Finished?" Then you pass it to somebody else. That other person is asked: "Do you have the instructions to the game? Now find monsters in those instructions so that if you needed to be instructed in that way you couldn't possibly make it out." Say we are going to propose a game of tic-tac-toe. Two persons play tic-tac-toe. Any two persons? When, today? Tomorrow? Do we have to be in sight of each other? Can we play by mail? Can one player be dead? This game is played on a board. It is chess. It is interesting that it is chess. I wonder what chess is. Is it a cylinder? Is it stacked? If the pieces are down, can I take all the pieces off before I begin and shake them up and then put them back on the board? . . . My classes can tell you that creating such problems is the easiest thing in the world. It comes off every time without fail. (Garfinkel's oral contributions in *Proceedings of The Purdue Symposium on Ethnomethodology*, edited by Richard J. Hill and Kathleen Stones Crittenden 1968, 211–12)

38. As Garfinkel points out:

> For example, although chess would seem to be immune to such manipulations, one can at one's move change pieces around on the board—so that, although the over-all positions are not changed, different pieces occupy the squares—and then move. On the several occasions in which I did this, my opponents were disconcerted, tried to stop me, demanded an explanation of what I was up to, were uncertain about the legality (but wanted to assert its illegality nevertheless), made it clear to me that I was spoiling the game for them, and at the next round of play made me promise that I would not "do anything this time." They were not satisfied when I asked that they point out where the rules prohibited what I had done. Nor were they satisfied when I pointed out that I had

not altered the material positions and, further, that the maneuver did not affect my chances of winning. If they were not satisfied, neither could they say to their satisfaction what was wrong. Prominently in their attempts to come to terms, they would speak of the obscurity of my motives. (1963, 199)

39. For examples of studies regarding this issue, see Zimmerman (1970) and Bittner (1965; 1967).

40. Cf. Also see, Wieder (1970, 233).

41. Cf. Zimmerman and Wieder (1970, 292).

42. In the Purdue Symposium, Garfinkel speaks of the basic rules as follows:

Now there is the crux of the matter. If we take those methods, we are dependent upon those methods. The adequacy of our translations now depends on a set of rules in terms of which correspondence is defined for its correctness, or is demonstrated, or seems correct. . . . What do those procedures consist of when you come to examine them as phenomena so that that reflexive character of these rule is apparent? To begin with, these rules have themselves properties of reportage. They have the features of "except," "unless," "let it pass," or "etc." (Garfinkel 1968, 27)

43. Cf. Speier (1973, 45–46) and Schenkein (1978).

44. Lynch (1993, 246). According to Lynch, this expression is taken from Garfinkel, Livingston, Lynch, and Robillard, "Respecifying the Natural Sciences as Discovering Sciences of Practical Action, Appendix I: Postscript and Preface (1989, 65)."

45. According to Lynch, due to this tendency of latter-day conversation analysis, "the rancor and mutual distancing" between formal analysis and ethnomethodology/conversation analysis appears to have subsided (1993, 272). See also, Alexander and Giesen (1987). They claim that the latter-day conversation analysis can be characterized as having a prominent tendency to approach micro-interactional practices by "constructing rules," that is, basic rules newly found by conversation analysis. Such rules can be incorporated within normative models of the social system (1987, 28). However, there are some different views of Lynch's criticism. See Psathas (1995b) and Clayman and Maynard (1995). They argue that conversation analysis shares ethnomethodology's originality because conversation analysis emphasizes the embodied order *in situ*.

46. To that extent, Lynch describes Garfinkel's ethnomethodology as follows: "What Garfinkel seemed to be suggesting was nothing less than an abandonment of a sociological 'core' in favor of an endless array of 'wild sociologies' existing beyond the pale of sociological empiricism" (1993, 272). For further discussion of "wild sociology," see John O'Neill (1980).

47. 'Fat moment' refers to a moment beyond the *hic et nunc*. In his Ph.D. dissertation, Garfinkel writes:

> A succession of . . . *fat moments* produces the notion of temporal sequence. But for playing in such [a] fast and loose [manner] with the relevance of time in the definition of action the fat moment squeezes out the temporal meaning of duration, so that one must look elsewhere than to the analysis of time to answer the question that remains: where to look for the factors that are conditional of the regularities of temporal succession? (1952, 147)

48. Lynch states:

> The *Lebenswelt* pair in mathematics may seem akin to other such "pairings" of documentary renderings with the lived work of some activity, but Garfinkel conjectures that "there exists, but only discoverably, and only for the natural sciences, domains of lebenswelt chemistry, lebenswelt physics, lebenswelt molecular biology, etc. just as there exists the discovered domain of lebenswelt mathematics" and, further, that "lebenswelt domains cannot be demonstrated for the social sciences" nor can they be demonstrated for various actions performed in accord with rules in games, manuals of instructions, contracts, and the like. (Lynch 1993, 294–95; Quoted from Garfinkel, Livingston, Lynch, and Robillard 1984, 128) See, also Livingston (1987, 119–126; 1986, 175–78).

49. Cf. Collins (1994, 275): "Society is full of illusions."

50. For an example of an ethnomethodological approach to mind, see Coulter (1991b; 1989; 1979).

51. In ethnomethodology "there is no conception of an 'inner dialogue' or an 'interiority of self'" (Watson 1998, 217). This does not mean that ethnomethodology and conversation analysis deny the existence of 'mental' or 'cognitive' phenomena, but rather that ethnomethodology and conversation analysis are concerned with these phenomena as publicly visible, witnessable, and manifest phenomena *in situ*.

52. Sacks defines membership categorization devices as "any collection of membership categories, containing at least a category, which may be applied to some population containing at least a member, so as to provide, by use of some rules of application, for the pairing of at least a population member and a categorization device member. A device is then a collection plus rules of application" (1974, 218–19).

BIBLIOGRAPHY

Ackerman, Charles, and Talcott Parsons. 1966. "The Concept of Social System as a Theoretical Device." In *Concepts, Theory and Explanation in the Behavioral Sciences*, edited by Gordon J. Di Renzo. New York: Random House.

Alexander, Jeffrey C. 1988. "Parsons' 'Structure' in American Sociology." *Sociological Theory* 6 (Spring):96–102.

———. 1987a. *Twenty Lectures: Sociological Theory Since World War II*. New York: Columbia University Press.

———. 1987b. "The Centrality of The Classics." In *Social Theory Today*, edited by Anthony Giddens and Jonathan H. Turner. Stanford, Calif.: Stanford University Press.

———. 1985. "The 'Individualist Dilemma' in Phenomenology and Interactionism." In *Macro-Sociological Theory: Perspectives on Sociological Theory*, Volume 1, edited by S.N. Eisenstadt and H.J. Helle. London: Sage Publications.

———. 1983. *Theoretical Logic in Sociology*. Vol.4, *The Modern Reconstruction of Classical Thought: Talcott Parsons*. Berkeley: University of California Press.

———. 1978. "Formal and Substantive Voluntarism in the Work of Talcott Parsons: A Theoretical and Ideological Reinterpretation." *American Sociological Review* 43:77–98.

Alexander, Jeffrey C., and B. Giesen. 1987. "From Reduction to Linkage: The Long View of the Micro-Macro Link." In *The Micro-Macro Link*, edited by J.C. Alexander, B. Giesen, R. Munch, and N.J. Smelser. Berkeley: University of California Press.

Anderson, R.J.; J.A. Hughes; and W.W. Sharrock. 1985. "The Relationship between Ethnomethodology and Phenomenology." *Journal of the British Society for Phenomenology* 16(3):221–35.

Antaki, C., and S. Widdicombe. 1998. "Identity as an Achievement and as a Tool." In *Identities in Talk*, edited by C. Antaki and S. Widdicombe. London: Sage Publications.

Arendt, Hannah. [1958] 1988. *The Human Condition*. Chicago: University of Chicago Press.

———. 1971. "Thinking and Moral Considerations: A Lecture." *Social Research* 38:418–46.

Atkinson, P. 1989. "Goffman's Poetics." *Human Studies* 12(1–2):59–76.

Baldmaus, W. 1972. "The Role of Discoveries in Social Science." In *The Rules of the Game*, edited by T. Shanin. London: Tavistock.

Battershill, C. 1990. "Erving Goffman as a Precursor to Post-Modern Sociology." In *Beyond Goffman*, edited by Stephen Harold Riggins. New York: Mouton de Gruyter.

Barnes, Barry. 1995. *The Elements of Social Theory*. Princeton, N.J.: Princeton University Press.

Becker, Howard. 1963. *Outsiders*. New York: Free Press.

Bell, Daniel. 1987. "The World and the United States in 2013." *Daedalus* 116(3): Summer:1–31.

Bellah, R.N.; N. Haan; P. Rainbow; and W.M. Sullivan, eds. 1983. *Social Science as Moral Inquiry*. New York: Columbia University Press.

Benjamin, Walter. 1969. *Illuminations*. Edited by Hannah Arendt. New York: Schocken Books.

Benson, Douglas, and John A. Hughes. 1983. *The Perspective of Ethnomethodology*. London: Longman.

Berard, Timothy James. 2000. The Micro-Politics of Macro-Categories: The Contested Relevance of Minority Status in Claims and Denials of Discrimination. Ph.D. diss., Boston University.

Berger, Peter L. 1997. *Redeeming Laughter: The Comic Dimension of Human Experience*. New York: Walter De Gruyter.

————. 1992. *A Far Glory: The Quest for Faith in an Age of Credulity.* New York: Anchor Books.

————. [1969] 1990. *A Rumor of Angels: Modern Society and the Rediscovery of the Supernatural.* New York: Doubleday.

————. 1980. Foreword to *Man in the Age of Technology,* by Arnold Gehlen. Translated by Patricia Lipscomb. New York: Columbia University Press.

————. 1979. *The Heretical Imperative: Contemporary Possibilities of Religious Affirmation.* Garden City, N.Y.: Anchor Book.

————. 1974. "Modern Identity: Crisis and Continuity." In *The Cultural Drama: Modern Identities and Social Ferment,* edited by Witon S. Dillon. Washington, D.C.: Smithsonian Institution Press.

————. 1973. "'Sincerity' and 'Authenticity' in Modern Society." *The Public Interest* 31: 81–90.

————. 1970a. "The Problems of Multiple Realities: Alfred Schutz and Robert Musil." In *Phenomenology and Social Reality,* edited by Maurice Natanson. The Hague: Nijhoff.

————. 1970b. "On the Obsolescence of the Concept of Honor." *European Journal of Sociology* 11:339–47.

————. 1967. *The Sacred Canopy: Elements of a Sociological Theory of Religion.* Garden City, N.Y.: Doubleday.

————. 1963. *Invitation to Sociology: A Humanistic Perspective.* Garden City, N.Y.: Doubleday.

————. 1961. *The Precarious Vision: A Sociologist Looks at Social Fictions and Christian Faith.* Garden City, N.Y.: Doubleday.

Berger, Peter, and Hansfried Kellner. 1981. *Sociology Reinterpreted: An Essay on Method and Vocation.* Garden City, N.Y.: Doubleday.

Berger, Peter; Brigitte Berger; and Hansfried Kellner. 1973. *The Homeless Mind: Modernization and Consciousness.* New York: Vintage Books.

Berger, Peter, and Richard J. Neuhaus. 1970. *Movement and Revolution.* Garden City, N.Y.: Doubleday.

Berger, Peter, and Thomas Luckmann. 1966. *The Social Construction of Reality: A Treatise in The Sociology of Knowledge.* Garden City, N.Y.: Doubleday.

Berger, Peter, and Hansfried Kellner. 1965. "Arnold Gehlen and The Theory of Institution." *Social Research* 32:110–15.

Berger, Peter, and Stanley Pullberg. 1965. "Reification and the Socio-logical Critique of Consciousness." *History and Theory* 4:196–211.

Berman, Marshall. 1988. *All That is Solid Melts into Air: The Experience of Modernity.* New York: Penguin Books.

Black, Max. 1961. *The Social Theories of Talcott Parsons.* Englewood Cliffs, N.J.: Prentice Hall.

Bittner, Egon. 1967. "The Police on Skid-Row: A Study of Peace Keep-ing." *American Sociological Review* 32:699–715.

———. 1965. "The Concept of Organization." *Social Research* 32: 230–55.

Boden, Deirdre, and Don H. Zimmerman., eds. 1991. *Talk and Social Structure: Studies in Ethnomethodology and Conversation Analysis.* Berkeley: University of California Press.

Boden, Deirdre, and Harvey Molotch. 1994. "The Compulsion of Prox-imity." In *NowHere: Space, Time, and Modernity*, edited by Roger Griedland and Deirdre Boden. Berkeley: University of California Press.

Bogen, David. 1993. "Order Without Rules: Wittgenstein and the Com-municative Ethics Controversy." *Sociological Theory* 11(1):55–71.

Boudon, Raymond. 1980. *The Crisis in Sociology: Problems of Sociological Epistemology.* Translated by Howard Davis. New York: Columbia University Press.

Bourricaud, François. [1977] 1981. *The Sociology of Talcott Parsons.* Chicago: University of Chicago Press.

Brittan, Arthur. 1977. *The Privatized World.* London: Routledge and Kegan Paul.

Burger, T. 1977. "Talcott Parsons, the Problem of Order in Society, and the Program of Analytic Sociology." *American Journal of Sociology* 81:320–34.

Burns, Tom. 1992. *Erving Goffman.* London: Routledge.

Button, Graham, ed. 1991. *Ethnomethodology and the Human Sciences.* Cambridge: Cambridge University Press.

Calinescu, Matei. 1987. *Five Faces of Modernity: Modernism, Avant-garde, Decadence, Kitsch, and Postmodernism.* Durham, N.C.: Duke Univer-sity Press.

Camic, C. 1989. "*Structure* after 50 Years: The Anatomy of a Charter." *American Journal of Sociology* 95(1):38–107.

Campbell, Colin. 1996. *The Myth of Social Action.* Cambridge: Cambridge University Press.

Cicourel, A.V. 1976. *The Social Organization of Juvenile Justice.* London: Heinemann.

Clark, Terry, ed. 1969. *Gabriel Tarde: On Communication and Social Influence.* Chicago: University of Chicago Press.

Clough, Patricia Ticineto. 1990. "Reading Goffman: Toward the Deconstruction of Sociology." In *Beyond Goffman*, edited by Stephen Harold Riggins. New York: Mouton de Gruyter.

Clayman, S. E., and D. Maynard. 1995. "Ethnomethodology and Conversation Analysis." In *Situated Order*, edited by Paul ten Have and George Psathas. Washington, D.C.: University Press of America.

Cohn, Stanley, and Laurie Taylor. 1976. *Escape Attempts: The Theory and Practice of Resistance to Everyday Life.* London: Routledge.

Collins, Randall. 1994. *Four Sociological Traditions.* Oxford: Oxford University Press.

———. 1988a. *Theoretical Sociology.* San Diego: Harcourt Brace Jovanovich.

———. 1988b. "Theoretical Continuities in Goffman's Work." In *Erving Goffman: Exploring the Interaction Order*, edited by Paul Drew and Anthony Wootton. Boston: Northeastern University Press.

———. 1986. "The Passing of Intellectual Generations: Reflections on the Death of Erving Goffman." *Sociological Theory* 4:106–13.

———. 1980. "Erving Goffman and the Development of Modern Social Theory." In *The View from Goffman*, edited by Jason Ditton. London: Macmillan.

Collins, Randall, and Michael Makowsky. 1972. "Erving Goffman and the Theatre of Social Encounters." *The Discovery of Society.* New York: Random House.

Coser, Rose Laub. 1991. *In Defense of Modernity: Role Complexity and Individual Autonomy.* Stanford, Calif.: Stanford University Press.

———. 1966. "Role Distance, Sociological Ambivalence and Traditional Status Systems." *American Journal of Sociology* 72:173–87.

Coser, Lewis. 1979. "A Dialogue of the Deaf." *Contemporary Sociology* 8(5):680–2.

Coulter, Jeff. 2001. "Human Practices and the Observability of the 'Macro-Social'." In *The Practice Turn in Contemporary Theory*, edited by Theodore R. Schatzki, Karin Knorr Cetina, and Eike von Savigny. London: Routledge.

———. 1996a. "Human Practices and the 'Micro-Macro' Link." Paper presented at conference, Practices and Social Order, 4–6 January, at Universität Bielefeld, Germany.

———. 1996b. "Chance, Cause and Conduct: Probability Theory and the Explanation of Human Action." In *Philosophy of Science, Logic, and Mathematics in the 20th Century*, edited by S. Shanker. New York: Routledge.

———. 1995. "Conceptual Transformations." *Sociological Theory* 13 (2):163–77.

———. 1991a. "Logic: Ethnomethodology and the Logic of Language." In *Ethnomethodology and The Human Sciences*, edited by G. Button. Cambridge: Cambridge University Press.

———. 1991b. "Cognition: Cognition in an Ethnomethodological Mode." In *Ethnomethodology and the Human Sciences*, edited by G. Button. Cambridge: Cambridge University Press.

———. 1989. *Mind in Action*. Atlantic Highlands: Humanities Press.

———. 1982. "Remarks on the Conceptualization of Social Structure." *Philosophy of Social Science* 12:33–46.

———, ed. 1980. *Ethnomethodological Studies. Human Studies* 3(1).

———. 1979. *The Social Construction of Mind: Studies in Ethnomethodology and Linguistic Philosophy*. Totowa, N.J.: Rowman and Littlefield.

Creelan, Paul. 1984. "Vicissitudes of the Sacred." *Theory and Society* 13(5):663–95.

Crook, Steve, and Laurie Taylor. 1980. "Goffman's version of Reality." In *The View from Goffman*, edited by Jason Ditton. London: Macmillan.

Cuff, E.C.; W. Sharrock; and D.W. Francis. 1992. *Perspectives in Sociology*. London: Routledge.

Cuzzort, Richard P. 1969. "Humanity as the Big Con: The Human Views of Erving Goffman." In *Humanity and Modern Sociological Thought*. New York: Holt, Rinehart and Winston.

Dallmayr, Fred. 1994. "Max Weber and the Modern State." In *The Barbarism of Reason: Max Weber and the Twilight of Enlightenment*, edited by Asher Horowitz and Terry Maley. Toronto: University of Toronto Press.

Davies, C. 1989. "Goffman's Concept of the Total Institution: Criticisms and Revisions." *Human Studies* 12(1–2):77–96.

Devereux, E.C. 1961. "Parsons' Sociological Theory." In *The Social Theories of Talcott Parsons*, edited by M. Black. Englewood Cliffs, N.J.: Prentice Hall.

Ditton, Jason, ed. 1980. *The View from Goffman*. London: Macmillan.

Drew, Paul, and Anthony Wootton. 1988. Introduction to *Erving Goffman: Exploring the Interaction Order*. Boston: Northeastern University Press.

Durkheim, Emile. "Individualism and the Intellectuals," In *Emile Durkheim on Morality and Society*, edited by R.N. Bellah. Chicago: University of Chicago Press.

———. 1964. *The Division of Labor in Society*. New York: Free Press.

———. 1951. *Suicide*. New York: Free Press.

Eliade, M. 1959. *The Sacred and the Profane: The Nature of Religion*, translated by Willard Trask. New York: Harcourt, Brace.

Fitzhenry, Roy. 1986. "Parsons, Schutz and the Problem of Verstehen." In *Talcott Parsons on Economy and Society*, edited by Robert J. Holton and Bryan S. Turner. London: Routledge.

Flynn, Pierce J. 1991. *The Ethnomethodological Movement: Sociosemiotic Interpretations*. New York: Mouton de Gruyter.

Fontana, Andrea. 1980. "The Mask and Beyond: The Enigmatic Sociology of Erving Goffman." *Introduction to the Sociologies of Everyday Life*, edited by Jack Douglas. Boston: Allyn & Bacon.

Freund, Julien. 1969. *The Sociology of Max Weber*. New York: Vintage.

Friedland, Roger, and Deirdre Boden. 1994. "NowHere: An Introduction to Space, Time and Modernity." In *NowHere: Space, Time and Modernity*, edited by Roger Friedland and Deirdre Boden. Berkeley: University of California Press.

Friedson, Eliot. 1983. "Celebrating Erving Goffman." *Contemporary Sociology* 12:359–362.

Frisby, David. 1986. *Fragments of Modernity.* Cambridge, Mass.: MIT Press.

Fromm, Erich. 1961. *Marx's Concept of Man.* New York: Frederick Ungar.

———. 1941. *Escape from Freedom.* New York: Rinehart.

Fuchs, Stephan. 1989. "Second Thought on Emergent Interaction Orders." *Sociological Theory* 7(1):121–3.

———. 1988. "The Constitution of Emergent Interaction Orders: A Comment on Rawls." *Sociological Theory* 1(1):122–4.

Gardner, Carol Brooks. 1994. "Out of Place: Gender, Public Places, and Situational Disadvantage." In *NowHere: Space, Time and Modernity*, edited by Roger Friedland and Deirdre Boden. Berkeley: University of California Press.

Garfinkel, Harold. 2001. "The Corpus Status of Ethnomethodological Investigation." Paper presented at Orders of Ordinary Action Conference, 9–11 July, Manchester Metropolitan University, UK.

———. 1996. "Ethnomethodology's Program." *Social Psychology Quarterly* 59(1):5–21.

———. 1991. "Respecification: Evidence for Locally Produced, Naturally Accountable Phenomena of Order*, Logic, Reason, Meaning, Method, etc. In and As of the Essential Haecceity of Immortal Ordinary Society, (I)—An Announcement of Studies." In *Ethnomethodology and the Human Sciences*, edited by G. Button. Cambridge: Cambridge University Press.

———. 1988. "Evidence for Locally Produced, Naturally Accountable Phenomena of Order*, Logic, Reason, Meaning, Method, etc. In and As of the Essential Quiddity of Immortal Ordinary Society, (I of IV): An Announcement of Studies." *Sociological Theory* 6:103–109.

———. 1977. "When is Phenomenology Sociological?" A panel discussion with J. O'Neill, G. Psathas, E. Rose, E. Tiryakian, H. Wagner, and D. L. Wieder. In *Annals of Phenomenological Sociology* 2:1–40.

———. 1974. "On the Origins of the Term 'Ethnomethodology.'" In *Ethnomethodology*, edited by R. Turner. Harmondsworth: Penguin.

———. 1968. "Oral Contributions." In *Proceedings of the Purdue Symposium on Ethnomethodology*, edited by R.J. Hill and K.S. Crittenden. Institute Monograph Series. No.1. West Lafayette, Ind.: Purdue University, Institute for the Study of Social Change.

———. 1967a. *Studies in Ethnomethodology.* Englewood Cliffs, N.J.: Prentice Hall.

———. 1967b. "Practical Sociological Reasoning: Some Features in the Work of the Los Angeles Suicide Prevention Center." In *Essays in Self-Destruction,* edited by E.S. Schneidman. New York: International Science Press.

———. 1963. "A Conception of, and Experiments with, 'Trust' as a Condition of Stable Concerted Actions." In *Motivation and Social Interaction,* edited by O.J. Harvey. New York: Ronald Press.

———. 1960. Parsons Primer. Unpublished draft from notes and transcripts of recorded meetings of a seminar conducted by Harold Garfinkel in the Department of Anthropology and Sociology, University of California, Los Angeles, Spring Semester, 1959: Sociology 251.

———. 1959. "Aspects of the Problem of Commonsense Knowledge of Social Structures." *Transactions of the Fourth World Congress of Sociology* 4:51–65.

———. 1956a. "Conditions of Successful Degradation Ceremonies." *American Journal of Sociology* 61:240–4.

———. 1956b. "Some Sociological Concepts and Methods for Psychiatrists." *Psychiatric Research Reports* 6:181–95.

———. 1952. *The Perception of the Other: A Study in Social Order.* Ph.D. diss., Harvard University.

Garfinkel, Harold, and D. Lawrence Wieder. 1992. "Two Incommensurable, Asymmetrically Alternate Technologies of Social Analysis." In *Text in Context: Contributions to Ethnomethodology,* edited by Graham Watson and Robert M. Seiler. London: Sage Publications.

Garfinkel, Harold; Lynch, M.; and Livingston, E. 1981. "The Work of a Discovering Science Construed with Materials from the Optically Discovered Pulsar." *Philosophy of the Social Sciences* 11:131–58.

Garfinkel, Harold, and H. Sacks. 1970. "On Formal Structures of Practical Actions." In *Theoretical Sociology,* edited by J.C. McKinney and E.A. Tiryakian. New York: Appleton Century Crofts.

Geertz, Clifford. 1983. *Local Knowledge.* New York: Basic Books.

Gehlen, Arnold. [1950] 1988. *Man: His Nature and Place in the World.* New York: Columbia University Press.

————. [1961] 1987. "The Crystallization of Cultural Forms." In *Modern German Sociology*, edited by Volker Meja, Dieter Misgeld, and Nico Stehr. New York: Columbia University Press.

————. [1957] 1980. *Man in the Age of Technology.* New York: Columbia University Press.

————. 1956. *Urmensch und Spätkultur.* Bonn: Athenaeum.

Giddens, Anthony. 1992. *The Transformation of Intimacy.* Stanford, Calif.: Stanford University Press.

————. 1991. *Modernity and Self-Identity.* Stanford, Calif.: Stanford University Press.

————. 1990. *The Consequences of Modernity.* Stanford, Calif.: Stanford University Press.

————. 1988. "Goffman as a Systematic Social Theorist." In *Erving Goffman: Exploring the Interaction Order*, edited by Paul Drew and Anthony Wootton. Boston: Northeastern University Press.

————. 1987. *Social Theory and Modern Sociology.* Cambridge: Polity Press.

————. 1984. *The Constitution of Society.* Cambridge: Polity Press.

————. 1983. *Profiles and Critiques in Social Theory.* Berkeley: University of California Press.

————. 1979. *Central Problems in Social Theory: Action, Structure and Contradiction in Social Analysis.* Berkeley: University of California Press.

Giddens, Anthony, and Jonathan H. Turner, eds. 1987. *Social Theory Today.* Stanford, Calif.: Stanford University Press.

Goffman, Erving. 1983a. "Felicity's Condition." *American Journal of Sociology* 89(1):1–53.

————. 1983b. "The Interaction Order." *American Sociological Review* 48(1):1–17.

————. 1981a. *Forms of Talk.* Oxford: Basil Blackwell.

————. 1981b. "Reply to Denzin and Keller." *Contemporary Sociology* 10(1):60–8.

————. 1979. *Gender Advertisements.* London: Macmillan.

————. 1974. *Frame Analysis: An Essay on the Organization of Experience.* New York: Harper & Row.

———. 1971. *Relations in Public: Microstudies of the Public Order.* New York: Basic Books.

———. 1970. *Strategic Interaction.* Oxford: Basil Blackwell.

———. 1967. *Interaction Ritual: Essays on Face-to-Face Behavior.* Garden City, New York: Anchor Books.

———. 1963a. *Behavior in Public Places: Notes on the Social Organization of Gatherings.* New York: Free Press.

———. 1963b. *Stigma: Notes on the Management of Spoiled Identity.* Englewood Cliffs, N.J.: Prentice Hall.

———. 1961a. *Asylums: Essays on the Social Situation of Mental Patients and Other Inmates.* Harmondsworth: Penguin.

———. 1961b. *Encounters: Two Studies in the Sociology of Interaction.* Indianapolis, Ind.: Bobbs-Merrill.

———. 1959. *The Presentation of Self in Everyday Life.* Harmondsworth: Penguin.

———. 1953. *Communication Conduct in an Island Community.* Ph.D. diss., University of Chicago.

———. 1952. "On Cooling the Mark Out: Some Aspects of Adaptation to Failure." *Psychiatry* 15(4):451–63.

———. 1951. "Symbols of Class Status." *British Journal of Sociology* 11:294–304.

Gonos, G. 1980. "The Class Position of Goffman's Sociology: Social Origins of an American Structuralism." In *The View from Goffman*, edited by Jason Ditton. London: Macmillan.

———. 1977. "Situation vs. Frame: The 'Interactionist' and the 'Structuralist' Analyses of Everyday Life." *American Sociological Review* 42(6):854–67.

Gould, Mark. 1991. "The Structure of Social Action: At Least Sixty Years Ahead of Its Time." In *Talcott Parsons: Theorist of Modernity*, edited by Roland Robertson and Bryan S. Turner. London: Sage Publications.

———. 1989. "Voluntarism versus Utilitarianism: A Critique of Camic's History of Ideas." *Theory, Culture and Society* 6(4):637–54.

Gouldner, Alvin. 1970. *The Coming Crisis in Western Sociology.* New York: Basic Books.

Grathoff, Richard. 1978. *The Theory of Social Action: The Correspondence of Alfred Schutz and Talcott Parsons*. Bloomington: Indiana University Press.

Grimshaw, Allen. 1983. "Erving Goffman: A Personal Appreciation." *Language in Society* 12(1):147–8.

Harbermas, Jürgen 1984. *The Theory of Communicative Action*. Boston: Beacon Press.

Haley, Peter. 1984. "Marx's Use of Images of the Profane." *Midwest Quarterly* 25(3):239–52.

Hamilton, P. 1983. *Talcott Parsons*. London: Ellis Horwood.

Heath, Christian. 1988. "Embarrassment and Interactional Organization." In *Erving Goffman: Exploring the Interaction Order*, edited by Paul Drew and Anthony Wootton. Boston: Northestern University Press.

Hepworth, Mike. 1980. "Deviance and Control in Everyday Life: The Contribution of Erving Goffman." In *The View from Goffman*, edited by Jason Ditton. London: Macmillan.

Heritage, John. 1987. "Ethnomethodology." In *Social Theory Today*, edited by Anthony Giddens and Jonathan Turner. Stanford, Calif.: Stanford University Press.

———. 1984. *Garfinkel and Ethnomethodology*. Cambridge: Polity Press.

Hester, Stephen. 1988. "Describing 'Deviance' in School." In *Identities in Talk*, edited by C. Antaki and S. Widdicombe. London: Sage Publications.

Hester, Stephen, and Peter Eglin. 1997. *Culture in Action: Studies in Membership Categorization Analysis*. Washington, D.C.: University Press of America.

———. 1992. *A Sociology of Crime*. London: Routledge.

Hilbert, Richard A. 1992. *The Classical Roots of Ethnomethodology: Durkheim, Weber, and Garfinkel*. Chapel Hill: University of North Carolina Press.

———. 1990. "Ethnomethodology and the Micro-Macro Order." *American Sociological Review* 55:794–808.

Hollis, M. 1985. "Of Masks and Men." In *The Category of the Person*, edited by M. Carrithers, S. Collins, and S. Lukes. Cambridge: Cambridge University Press.

Holton, Robert. 1986. "Talcott Parsons and the Theory of Economy and Society." In *Talcott Parsons on Economy and Society*, edited by Robert Holton and Bryan S. Turner. London: Routledge.

Holton, Robert, and Bryan S. Turner. 1986a. "Reading Talcott Parsons: Introductory Remarks." In *Talcott Parsons on Economy and Society*, edited by Robert Holton and Bryan S. Turner. London: Routledge.

———. 1986b. "Against Nostalgia: Talcott Parsons and a Sociology for the Modern World." In *Talcott Parsons on Economy and Society*, edited by Robert Holton and Bryan S. Turner. London: Routledge.

Hopper, R. 1991. "Hold the Phone." In *Talk and Social Structure*, edited by D. Boden and D. Zimmerman. Berkeley: University of California Press.

Horowitz, Asher. 1994. "The Comedy of Enlightenment: Weber, Habermas, and the Critique of Reification." In *The Barbarism of Reason: Max Weber and the Twilight of Enlightenment*, edited by Asher Horowitz and Terry Maley. Toronto: University of Toronto Press.

Horowitz, Asher, and Terry Maley. 1994. Introduction to *The Barbarism of Reason: Max Weber and the Twilight of Enlightenment*, edited by Asher Horowitz and Terry Maley. Toronto: University of Toronto Press.

Jayyusi, Lena. 1984. *Categorization and the Moral Order*. Boston: Routledge and Kegan Paul.

Jenkins, Richard. 1996. *Social Identity*. London: Routledge

Joas, Hans. 1993. *Pragmatism and Social Theory*. Chicago: University of Chicago Press.

———. 1985. "Role Theories and Socialization Research." In *Micro-Sociological Theory: Perspectives on Sociological Theory*, Vol. 2, edited by H.J. Helle and S.N. Eisenstadt. London: Sage Publications.

Johnson, Peter. 1993. *Frames of Deceit: A Study of the Loss and Recovery of Public and Private Trust*. Cambridge: Cambridge University Press.

Jules-Rosette, Bennetta. 1980. "Talcott Parsons and the Phenomenological Tradition in Sociology: An Unresolved Debate." *Human Studies* 3(4):311–30.

Kalberg, Stephen. 2000. "Max Weber." In *The Blackwell Companion to Major Social Theorists*, edited by George Ritzer. Malden, Mass.: Blackwell.

Kellner, Douglas. 1992. "Popular Culture and the Construction of Postmodern Identities." In *Modernity and Identity*, edited by Scott Lash and Jonathan Friedman. Oxford: Blackwell.

Kendon, Adam. 1988. "Goffman's Approach to Face-to-Face Interaction." In *Erving Goffman: Exploring the Interaction Order*, edited by Paul Drew and Anthony Wootton. Boston: Northeastern University Press.

Knorr-Centina, K., and Aaron Cicourel. 1981. *Advances in Social Theory and Methodology*. Boston: Routledge and Kegan Paul.

Kolb, D. 1986. *The Critique of Pure Modernity*. Chicago: University of Chicago Press.

Kroeber, A.C., and Talcott Parsons. 1958. "The Profession: Reports and Opinion: The Concepts of Culture and of Social System." *American Sociological Review* 23(5):582–3.

LaCapra, Dominick. 1972. *Emile Durkheim: Sociologist and Philosopher*. Ithaca, N.Y.: Cornell University Press.

Lasch, Christopher. 1985. *The Minimal Self*. London: Picador.

———. 1980. *The Culture of Narcissism*. London: Abacus.

Lash, Scott, and Jonathan Freidman. 1992. *Modernity and Identity*. Oxford: Backwell.

Lechner, Frank J. 1991. "Parsons and Modernity: An Interpretation." In *Talcott Parsons: Theorist of Modernity*, edited by Roland Robertson and Bryan S. Turner. London: Sage Publications.

Lee, J.R.E. 1987. "Prologue: Talking Organization." In *Talk and Social Organization*, edited by Graham Button and J.R.E. Lee. Clevedon: Multilingual Matters.

Leiter, Kenneth. 1980. *A Primer on Ethnomethodology*. Oxford: Oxford University Press.

Lemert, Charles C. 1995. *Sociology: After the Crisis*. Boulder, Colo.: Westview.

———. 1979. *Sociology and the Twilight of Man: Homocentrism and Discourse in Sociological Theory*. Carbondale: Southern Illinois University Press.

Levin, Donald N. 1991. "Simmel and Parsons Reconsidered." In *Talcott Parsons: Theorist of Modernity*, edited by Roland Robertson and Bryan S. Turner. London: Sage Publications.

Levinson, Stephen C. 1988. "Putting Linguistics on a Proper Footing: Explorations in Goffman's Concepts of Participation." In *Erving Goffman: Exploring the Interaction Order*, edited by Paul Drew and Anthony Wootton. Boston: Northeastern University Press.

Lidz, Victor. 1991a. "The American Value System: A Commentary on Talcott Parson's Perspective and Understanding." In *Talcott Parsons: Theorist of Modernity*, edited by Roland Robertson and Bryan S. Turner. London: Sage Publicatons.

———. 1991b. "Influence and Solidarity: Defining a Conceptual Core for Sociology." In *Talcott Parsons: Theorist of Modernity*, edited by Roland Robertson and Bryan S. Turner. London: Sage Publications.

Livingston, Eric. 1987. *Making Sense of Ethnomethodology*. London: Routledge & Kegan Paul.

———. 1986. *The Ethnomethodological Foundations of Mathematics*. London: Routledge and Kegan Paul.

Lofland, John. 1980. "Early Goffman: Style, Structure, Substance, Soul." In *The View from Goffman*, edited by Jason Ditton. London: Macmillan.

Luckmann, Thomas. [1979] 1987. "Personal Identity as an Evolutionary and Historical Problem." In *Modern German Sociology*, edited by Volker Meja, Dieter Misgeld, and Nico Stehr. New York: Columbia University Press.

———. 1983. *Life-World and Social Realities*. London: Heinemann.

———. 1967. *The Invisible Religion: The Problem of Religion in Modern Society*. New York: Macmillan.

———. 1963. "On Religion in Modern Society." *Journal for the Scientific Study of Religion* 2(2):147–62.

Lukes, Steven. 1967. "Alienation and Anomie." *Philosophy, Politics and Society* 3:134–56.

Lyman, Stanford M. 1990. "The Drama in the Routine: A Prolegomenon to a Praxiological Sociology." *Sociological Theory* 8(2): 217–23.

Lynch, Michael. 2001. "Ethnomethodology and the Logic of Practice." In *The Practice Turn in Contemporary Theory*, edited by Theodore R. Schatzki, Karin Knorr Cetina, and Eike von Savigny. London: Routledge.

———. 1997. "Silence in Context: Ethnomethodology at the Margin of Social Theory." Paper presented at the Conference, Ethnomethodology East and West. 20–22 August. Waseda University, Tokyo, Japan.

———. 1993. *Scientific Practice and Ordinary Action: Ethnomethodology and Social Studies of Science.* Cambridge: Cambridge University Press.

Lynch, Michael; Eric Livingston; and Harold Garfinkel. 1983. "Temporal Order in Laboratory Work." In *Science Observed: Perspectives on the Social Study of Science,* edited by Karin D. Knorr-Centina, and Michael Mulkay. London: Sage Publications.

MacCannell, Dean. 1990. "The Descent of the Ego." In *Beyond Goffman,* edited by Stephen Harold Riggins. New York: Mouton de Gruyter.

———. 1983. "Erving Goffman (1922–1982)." *Semiotica* 45:1–33.

MacIntyre, Alasdair. 1981. *After Virtue.* Brighton: Duckworth.

———. 1969. "The Self as Work of Art." *New Statesman.* 28 March.

Maley, Terry. 1994. "The Politics of Time: Subjectivity and Modernity in Max Weber." In *The Barbarism of Reason: Max Weber and the Twilight of Enlightenment,* edited by Asher Horowitz and Terry Maley. Toronto: University of Toronto Press.

Manning, Peter K. 1980. "Goffman's Framing Order: Style as Structure." In *The View from Goffman,* edited by Jason Ditton. London: Macmillan.

Manning, Phil. 1992. *Erving Goffman and Modern Sociology.* Stanford, Calif.: Stanford University Press.

———. 1991. "Drama as Life: The Significance of Goffman's Changing Use of the Theatrical Metaphor." *Sociological Theory* 9(1):70–86.

Marx, Gary T. 1984. "Role Models and Role Distance: A Remembrance of Erving Goffman." *Theory and Society* 13(5):649–62.

Marx, Karl. [1844] 1978. "Economic and Philosophic Manuscripts of 1844." In *The Marx-Engels Reader.* 2nd ed. Edited by Robert C. Tucker. New York: W.W. Norton.

———. [1844] 1961. "Economic and Philosophic Manuscripts of 1844." Translated by T.B. Bottomore. In *Marx's Concept of Man,* by Erich Fromm. New York: Frederick Ungar.

———. [1846–47] 1977. "The Poverty of Philosophy." In *Karl Marx: Selected Writings*, edited by David McLellan. Oxford: Oxford University Press.

Marx, Karl, and Friedrich Engels. [1847–48] 1967. *The Communist Manifesto*. Translated by Samuel Moore. New York: Penguin Books.

Maynard, Douglas W. 1996. "Introduction of Harold Garfinkel for the Cooley-Mead Award." *Social Psychology Quarterly* 59(1):1–4.

Maynard, Douglas W., and S.E. Clayman. 1991. "The Diversity of Ethnomethodology." *Annual Review of Sociology* 17:385–418.

Maynard, Douglas W., and T. Wilson. 1980. "On the Reification of Social Structure." *Current Perspectives in Social Theory* 1:287–322.

Mehan, Hugh, and Houston Wood. 1975. "An Image of Man for Ethnomethodology." *Philosophy of Social Science* 5:365–76.

Meyrowitz, Joshua. 1985. *No Sense of Place*. New York: Oxford University Press.

Miller, Thomas. 1984. "Goffman, Social Acting and Moral Behavior." *Journal for the Theory of Social Behaviour* 14(2):141–63.

Mouzelis, Nicos. 1995. *Sociological Theory: What Went Wrong?* London: Routledge.

Münch, Richard. 1987. "Parsonian Theory Today: In Search of a New Synthesis." In *Social Theory Today*, edited by Anthony Giddens and Jonathan Turner. Stanford, Calif.: Stanford University Press.

———. 1986. "The American Creed in Sociological Theory: Exchange, Negotiated Order, Accommodated Individualism, and Contingency." *Sociological Theory* 4(Spring):41–60.

———. 1982. "Talcott Parsons and the Theory of Action. II. The Continuity of the Development." *American Journal of Sociology* 87:771–826.

———. 1981. "Talcott Parsons and the Theory of Action. I. The Structure of the Kantian Core." *American Journal of Sociology* 86:709–39.

Musil, Robert. [1952] 1996. *The Man Without Qualities*. Translated by Sophie Wilkins. New York: Vintage.

Natanson, Maurice. 1998. "Alfred Schutz: Philosopher and Social Scientist." *Human Studies* 21(1):1–12.

———. 1986. *Anonymity: A Study in the Philosophy of Alfred Schutz.* Bloomington: Indiana University Press.

———. 1979. "Phenomenology, Anonymity, and Alienation." *New Literary History* 10(3):532–46.

———. 1978. "The Problem of Anonymity in the Thought of Alfred Schutz." In *Phenomenology and the Social Sciences: A Dialogue,* edited by Joseph Bien. The Hague: Nijhoff.

———. 1977. "Alfred Schutz Symposium: The Pregivenness of Sociality." In *Interdisciplinary Phenomenology,* edited by Don Ihde and Richard M. Zaner. The Hague: Martinus Nijhoff.

———. 1975. "The Problem of Anonymity in Gurwitsch and Schutz." *Research in Phenomenology* 5:51–6.

———. 1974. *Phenomenology, Role, and Reason: Essays on the Coherence and Deformation of Social Reality.* Springfield, Ill.: Charles C Thomas.

———. 1970a. *The Journeying Self: A Study in Philosophy and Social Role.* Reading, Mass.: Addison-Wesley.

———, ed. 1970b. *Phenomenology and Social Reality: Essays in Memory of Alfred Schutz.* The Hague: Nijhoff.

Nelson, Benjamin. 1969. *The Idea of Usury: From Tribal Brotherhood to Universal Otherhood.* Chicago: University of Chicago Press.

Ollman, Bertell. 1971. *Alienation: Marx's Concept of Man in Capitalist Society.* Cambridge: Cambridge University Press.

Olsen, Marvin E. 1965. "Durkheim's Two Concepts of Anomie." *Sociological Quarterly.* 6:37–44.

Ortega y Gasset, José. 1964. *The Revolt of the Masses.* New York: W.W. Norton.

Owen, David. 1994. *Maturity and Modernity; Nietzsche, Weber, Foucault and the Ambivalence of Reason.* London: Routledge.

Parsons, Talcott. 1991a. "A Tentative Outline of American Values." In *Talcott Parsons: Theorist of Modernity,* edited by Roland Robertson and Bryan Turner. London: Sage Publications.

———. 1991b. *The Early Essays.* Edited by Charles Camic. Chicago: University of Chicago Press.

———. 1982. *On Institutions and Social Evolution: Selected Writings.* Edited by Leon H. Mayhew. Chicago: University of Chicago Press.

———. 1978. *Action Theory and the Human Condition*. New York: Free Press.

———. 1978. "A Sociological and Action Perspective." *Encyclopedia of Bioethics* Vol. 2. New York: Free Press.

———. 1977. *Social Systems and the Evolution of Action Theory*. New York: Free Press.

———. 1974. "Comment on: 'Current Folklore in the Criticisms of Parsonian Action Theory.'" *Sociological Inquiry* 44(1):55–8.

———. 1973. "Culture and Social System Revisited." In *The Idea of Culture in the Social Sciences*, edited by Louis Schneider and Charles M. Bonjean. Cambridge: Cambridge University Press.

———. 1971. *The System of Modern Societies*. Englewood Cliffs, N.J.: Prentice Hall.

———. 1970. "Some Problems of General Theory in Sociology." In *Theoretical Sociology: Perspectives and Developments*, edited by J. McKinney and E. Tiryakian. New York: Appleton Century Crofts.

———. 1969. *Politics and Social Structure*. New York: Free Press.

———. 1967. *Sociological Theory and Modern Society*. New York: Free Press.

———. 1966. *Societies: Evolutionary and Comparative Perspectives*. Englewood Cliffs, N.J.: Prentice Hall.

———. 1964. *Social Structure and Personality*. Glencoe, Ill.: Free Press.

———. 1963. "Christianity and Modern Industrial Society." In *Sociological Theory, Values, and Sociocultural Change: Essays in Honor of Pitrim A. Sorokin*, edited by Edward A. Tiryakian. Glencoe, Ill.: Free Press.

———. 1962. "Individual Autonomy and Social Pressure: An Answer to Dennis Wrong." *Psychoanalysis and Psychoanalytic Review* 49 (2):70–9.

———. 1961. "An Outline of the Social System." In *Theories of Society: Foundations of Modern Sociological Theory*, edited by Talcott Parsons, E. Shils, K.D. Naegele, and, J.R. Pitts. Glencoe, Ill.: Free Press.

———. 1960. *Structure and Process in Modern Societies*. Glencoe, Ill.: Free Press.

———. 1959. "An Approach to Psychological Theory in Terms of the Theory of Action." In *Psychology: A Study of a Science*. Vol. 3:

Formulations of the Person and the Social Context, edited by Sigmund Koch. New York: McGraw-Hill.

————. 1958. "The Profession: Reports and Opinion." *American Sociological Review* 23(5):582–3.

————. 1954. *Essays in Sociological Theory*. Glencoe, Ill.: Free Press.

————. 1951. *The Social System*. Glencoe, Ill.: Free Press.

————. 1937. *The Structure of Social Action*. New York: McGraw-Hill.

Parsons, Talcott, and Gerald M. Platt. 1973. *The American University*. Cambridge, Mass.: Harvard University Press.

Parsons, Talcott, and W. White. 1960. "Commentary on the Mass Media and the Structure of American Society." *Journal of Social Issues* 16 (3):67–77.

Parsons, Talcott, and Neil J. Smelser. 1956. *Economy and Society: A Study in the Integration of Economic and Social Theory*. Glencoe, Ill.: Free Press.

Parsons, Talcott, and R.F. Bales, 1955. *Family, Socialization and Interaction Process*. Glencoe, Ill.: Free Press.

Parsons, Talcott; R.F. Bales; and E.A. Shils. 1953. *Working Papers in the Theory of Action*. Glencoe, Ill.: Free Press.

Parsons, Talcott, and Edward A. Shils, ed. 1951. *Toward a General Theory of Action*. Cambridge, Mass.: Harvard University Press.

Pickering, W.S.F. 1984. *Durkheim's Sociology of Religion: Themes and Theories*. Boston: Routledge & Kegan Paul.

Plessner, Helmut. 1978. "With Different Eyes." In *Phenomenology and Sociology*, edited by Thomas Luckmann. New York: Penguin.

Psathas, George. 1995a. *Conversation Analysis: The Study of Talk-in-Interaction*. London: Sage Publications.

————, ed. 1995b. *Ethnomethodology: Discussions and Contributions*. In *Human Studies* 18(2–3).

————, ed. 1990. *Interaction Competence*. Washington, D.C.: University Press of America.

————. 1994. "Ethnomethodology." *Encyclopedia of Language and Linguistics*. Oxford: Pergamon.

————. 1989. *Phenomenology and Sociology: Theory and Research*. Washington, D.C.: University Press of America.

———. 1980a. "Early Goffman and the Analysis of Face-to-Face Interaction in Strategic Interaction." In *The View from Goffman,* edited by Jason Ditton. London: Macmillan.

———. 1980b. "Approaches to the Study of the World of Everyday Life." *Human Studies* 3:3–17.

———, ed. 1979. *Everyday Language: Studies in Ethnomethodology.* New York: Irvington.

———. 1977a. "Ethnomethodology as a Phenomenological Approach in the Social Sciences." In *Interdisciplinary Phenomenology,* edited by Don Ihde and Richard M. Zaner. The Hague: Nijhoff.

———. 1977b. "Goffman's Image of Man." *Humanity and Society* 1 (1):84–94.

———. 1976. "Misinterpreting Ethnomethodology." Paper presented at the annual meeting of the American Sociological Association.

———, ed. 1973. *Phenomenological Sociology: Issues and Applications.* New York: John Wiley & Sons.

Rank, Otto. 1971. *The Double: A Psychoanalytic Study.* Chapel Hill: University of North Carolina Press.

Rawls, A. 2000. "Harold Garfinkel." In *The Blackwell Companion to Major Social Theorists,* edited by George Ritzer. Malden, Mass.: Blackwell.

———. 1989a. "An Ethnomethodological Perspective on Social Theory." In *The Interactional Order: New Directions in the Study of Social Order,* edited by D.T. Helm, W.T. Anderson, A.J. Meehan and A. Rawls. New York: Irvington.

———. 1989b. "Language, Self, and Social Order." *Human Studies* 12(1–2):147–72.

———. 1989c. "Simmel, Parsons and the Interaction Order." *Sociological Theory* 7(Spring):124–9.

———. 1988. "Interaction vs. Interaction Order: Reply to Fuchs." *Sociological Theory* 6(1):124–9.

———. 1987. "The Interaction Order Sui Generis: Goffman's Contribution to Social Theory." *Sociological Theory* 5(2):136–49.

Riggins, Stephen H., ed. 1990. *Beyond Goffman: Studies on Communication, Institution, and Social Interaction.* Berlin: Mouton de Gruyter.

Robertson, Roland, and Bryan S. Turner. 1991. "An Introduction to Talcott Parsons: Theory, Politics and Humanity." In *Talcott Parsons,*

Theorist of Modernity, edited by Roland Robertson and Bryan S. Turner. London: Sage Publications.

Robillard, Albert B. 1999. "Wild Phenomena and Disability Jokes." *Body & Society* 5(4):61–5.

Rocher, G. 1974. *Talcott Parsons and American Sociology*. London: Nelson.

Roger, Mary. 1980. "Goffman on Power, Hierarchy, and Status." In *The View from Goffman*, edited by Jason Ditton. London: Macmillan.

Roth, Andrew. 1995. "Men Wearing Masks: Issues of Description in the Analysis of Ritual." *Sociological Theory* 13(3):301–27.

Ryan, Alan. 1978. "Maximising, Minimising, Moralizing." In *Action and Interpretation*, edited by C. Hookway and P. Petitt. Cambridge: Cambridge University Press.

Sartre, Jean-Paul. 1956. *Being and Nothingness*. Translated by Hazel E. Barnes. New York: Philosophical Library.

Sacks, Harvey. 1992. *Lectures on Conversation*. Volumes I & II. Edited by Gail Jefferson. Oxford: Blackwell.

———. 1984. "Notes on Methodology." In *Structures of Social Action*, edited by J.M. Atkinson and J. Heritage. Cambridge: Cambridge University Press.

———. 1974. "On the Analyzability of Stories by Children." In *Ethnomethodology*, edited by Roy Turner. Harmondworth: Penguin.

———. 1972. "An Initial Investigation of the Usability of Conversational Data for Doing Sociology." In *Studies in Social Interaction*, edited by D. Sudnow. New York: Free Press.

Sacks, Harvey, and E. A. Schegloff. 1979. "Two Preferences in the Organization of Reference to Persons in Conversation and Their Interaction." In *Everyday Language*, edited by George Psathas. New York: Irvington.

Sacks, Harvey; E. Schegloff; and G. Jefferson. 1974. "A Simplest Systematics for the Organization of Turntaking in Conversation." *Language* 50(4):696–735.

Scaff, Lawrence A. 1989. *Fleeing the Iron Cage: Culture, Politics, and Modernity in the Thought of Max Weber*. Berkeley: University of California Press.

Scheff, Thomas J. 1990. *Microsociology: Discourse, Emotion, and Social Structure*. Chicago: University of Chicago Press.

Schegloff, Emanuel A. 1988. "Goffman and the Analysis of Conversation." In *Erving Goffman: Exploring the Interaction Order*, edited by Paul Drew and Anthony Wootton. Boston: Northeastern University Press.

Schegloff, Emanuel A., and H. Sacks. 1974. "Opening Up Closings." In *Ethnomethodology*, edited by R. Turner. Harmondsworth: Penguin.

Schelling, T. 1960. *The Strategy of Conflict.* Cambridge, Mass.: Harvard University Press.

Schelsky, Helmut. [1959] 1987. "Sociology as a Science of Social Reality." In *Modern German Sociology*, edited by Volker Meja, Dieter Msgeld, and Nico Stehr. New York: Columbia University Press.

———. 1965. "Ist die Dauerreflexion institutionalisierbar?" In *Auf der Suche nach Wirklichkeit.* Düsseldorf: Diederichs.

Schenkein, J., ed. 1978. *Studies in the Organization of Conversational Interaction.* New York: Academic Press.

Schudson, Michael. "Embarrassment and Erving Goffman's idea of Human Nature." *Theory and Society* 13(5):633–48.

Schutz, Alfred. 1967. *The Phenomenology of the Social World.* Translated by George Walsh and Frederick Lehnert. Evanston, Ill.: Northwestern University Press.

———. 1964. *Collected Papers.* Vol. II: *Studies in Social Theory.* The Hague: Nijhoff.

———. 1964b. "The Stranger." In *Collected Papers.* Vol. II: *Studies in Social Theory.* The Hague: Nijhoff.

———. 1962. *Collected Papers.* Vol. I: *The Problem of Social Reality.* The Hague: Nijhoff.

Schwanenberg, E. 1970. "The Two Problems of Order in Parsons' Theory." *Social Forces* 49:569–81.

Scott, John Finley. 1974. "Interpreting Parsons' Work: A Problem in Method." *Sociological Inquiry* 44(1):58–61.

Seidman, Steven. 1983a. "Modernity, Meaning, and Cultural Pessimism in Max Weber." *Sociological Analysis* 44(4):267–78.

———. 1983b. "Modernity and the Problem of Meaning: The Durkheimian Tradition." *Sociological Analysis* 46:109–30.

Seligman, Adam B. 2000. *Modernity's Wager: Authority, the Self, and Transcendence.* Princeton, N.J.: Princeton University Press.

——. 1997. *The Problem of Trust.* Princeton, N.J.: Princeton University Press.

Sennett, Richard. 1977. *The Fall of Public Man.* Cambridge: Cambridge University Press.

Sharrock, Wes, and G. Button. 1991. "The Social Actor: Social Action in Real Time." In *Ethnomethodology and the Human Sciences,* edited by G. Button. Cambridge: Cambridge University Press.

Sharrock, Wes, and Bob Anderson. 1986. *The Ethnomethodologists.* London: Tavistock.

Sharrock, Wes, and D.R. Watson. 1988. "Autonomy among Social Theories: The Incarnation of Social Structure." In *Actions and Structure: Research Methods and Social Theory,* edited by N.G. Fieding. London: Sage Publications.

Simmel, Georg. 1978. *The Philosophy of Money.* Edited and translated by David Frisby. London: Routledge.

——. 1950a. "The Stranger." In *The Sociology of Georg Simmel,* edited by Kurt H. Wolff. Glencoe, Ill.: Free Press.

——. 1950b. "The Metropolis and Mental Life." In *The Sociology of Georg Simmel,* edited by Kurt H. Wolff. Glencoe, Ill.: Free Press.

Smart, Barry. 1999. *Facing Modernity: Ambivalence, Reflexivity and Morality.* London: Sage Publications.

Smith, G.W.H. 1989. "Snapshots 'sub specie aeternitatis': Simmel, Goffman and Formal Sociology." *Human Studies* 12(1–2):19–58.

Speier, M. 1973. *How to Observe Face-to-Face Communication.* Pacific Palisades, Calif.: Goodyear.

Stebbins, Robert A. 1967. "A Note on the Concept Role Distance." *American Journal of Sociology* 73:247–50.

Stern, Fritz. *The Failure of Illiberalism.* New York: Knopf.

Strong, P.M. 1988. "Minor Courtesies and Macro Structures." In *Erving Goffman: Exploring the Interaction Order,* edited by Paul Drew and Anthony Wootton. Boston: Northeastern University Press.

Sudnow, David, ed. *Studies in Social Interaction.* New York: Free Press.

Ten Have, Paul, and George Psathas, ed. 1995. *Situated Order: Studies in the Social Organization of Talk and Embodied Activities.* Washington, D.C.: University Press of America.

Taylor, Charles. 1975. *Hegel.* Cambridge: Cambridge University Press.

Thomas, W.I. [1928] 1967. *The Unadjusted Girl.* New York: Harper Torchbooks.

Tiryakian, Edward A. 1981. "The Sociological Input of a Metaphor: Tracking the Source of Max Weber's 'Iron Cage'." *Sociological Inquiry* 51:7–33.

Trilling, Lionel. 1972. *Sincerity and Authenticity.* Cambridge, Mass.: Harvard University Press.

Turner, Bryan S. 1986a. "Sickness and Social Structure: Parsons' Contribution to Medical Sociology." In *Talcott Parsons on Economy and Society,* edited by Robert Holton and Bryan S. Turner. London: Routledge.

———. 1986b. "Parsons and His Critics: On the Ubiquity of Functionalism." In *Talcott Parsons on Economy and Society,* edited by Robert Holton and Bryan S. Turner. London: Routledge.

Turner, Jonathan. 1988. *A Theory of Social Interaction.* Stanford, Calif.: Stanford University Press.

———. 1974. *The Structure of Sociological Theory.* Homewood, Ill.: Dorsey Press.

Turner, Jonathan, and Leonard Beeghley. 1974. "Current Folklore in the Criticisms of Parsonian Action Theory." *Sociological Inquiry* 44 (1):47–63.

Turner, Ralph H. 1962. "Role-Taking: Process Versus Conformity." In *Human Behavior and Social Process,* edited by A. M. Rose. London: Routledge.

———. 1955. "Role-Taking, Role-Standpoint, and Reference-Group Behavior." *American Journal of Sociology* 61:316–28.

Turner, Roy, ed. 1974. *Ethnomethodology.* Harmondsworth: Penguin.

Verhoeven, Jef. 1985. "Goffman's Frame Analysis and Modern Micro-Sociological Paradigms." In *Micro-Sociological Theory: Perspectives on Sociological Theory.* Vol. 2, edited by H.J. Helle and S.N. Eisenstadt. London: Sage Publications.

Vogelin, Eric. 1970. "The Eclipse of Reality." In *Phenomenology and Social Reality: Essays in Memory of Alfred Schutz*, edited by Maurice Natanson. The Hague: Nijhoff.

Waksler, Frances Chaput. 1989. "Erving Goffman's Sociology: An Introductory Essay." *Human Studies* 12(1–2):1–18.

Walsh, David. 1972. "Functionalism and Systems Theory." In *New Directions in Sociological Theory*, edited by Paul Filmer. Michael Phillipson; David Silverman; and David Walsh. Cambridge, Mass.: The MIT Press.

Watson, Graham, and Robert M. Seiler, ed. 1992. *Text in Context: Contributions to Ethnomethodology*. Newbury Park, Calif.: Sage Publications.

Weber, Max. 2001. *The Protestant Ethic and the Spirit of Capitalism.* Translated by Stephen Kalberg. Los Angeles, Calif.: Roxbury.

———. 1963. *The Sociology of Religion*. Boston: Beacon Press.

———. 1946. *From Max Weber: Essays on Sociology*. Translated and edited by G.H. Gerth and C.W. Mills. Boston: Routledge and Kegan Paul.

Weil, Simone. 1963. *Gravity and Grace*. London: Routledge and Kegan Paul.

Whalen, J. 1991. "Conversation Analysis." In *The Encyclopedia of Sociology*, edited by E.F. Borgatta and M.C. Borgatta. New York: Macmillan.

Wieder, D.L. 1988. *Language and Social Reality*. Washington, D.C.: University Press of America.

———. 1974. "Telling the Code." In *Ethnomethodology*, edited by R. Turner. Middlesex: Penguin.

Wiliams, Robin. 1988. "Understanding Goffman's Methods." In *Erving Goffman: Exploring the Interaction Order*, edited by Paul Drew and Anthony Wootton. Boston: Northeastern University Press.

———. 1980. "Goffman's Sociology of Talk." In *The View from Goffman*, edited by Jason Ditton. London: Macmillan.

Wilson, T.P. 1991. "Social Structure and the Sequential Organization of Interaction." In *Talk and Social Structure*, edited by D. Boden and D. Zimmerman. Berkeley: University of California Press.

Wilson, T.P., and D. Zimmerman. 1980. "Ethnomethodology, Sociology, and Theory." *Humboldt Journal of Social Relations* 7:52–88.

Wrong, Dennis H. 1994. *The Problem of Order: What Unites and Divides Society.* New York: Free Press.

————. 1961. "The Oversocialized Conception of Man in Modern Sociology." *American Sociological Review* 26(2):183–93.

Zijderveld, Anton C. 1998. *A Theory of Urbanity: The Economic and Civic Culture of Cities.* New Brunswick, N.J.: Transaction publishers.

————. 1982. *Reality in A Looking-Glass: Rationality Through an Analysis of Traditional Folly.* London: Routledge and Kegan Paul.

————. 1979. *On Cliché: The Supersedure of Meaning by Function in Modernity.* London: Routledge and Kegan Paul.

————. 1972. "The Anti-Institutional Mood." *Worldview* 15(9) Sept., 32–36.

————. 1970. *The Abstract Society: A Cultural Analysis of Our Time.* Garden City, N.Y.: Anchor Books.

Zimmerman, Don. 1998. "Identity, Context, and Interaction." In *Identities in Talk*, edited by C. Antaki and S. Widdicombe. London: Sage Publications.

————. 1970. "The Practicalities of Rule Use." In *Understanding Everyday Life*, edited by J. Douglas. Chicago: Aldine.

Zimmerman, Don, and Melvin Pollner. 1970. "The Everyday World as a Phenomenon." In *Understanding Everyday Life*, edited by J. Douglas. Chicago: Aldine.

NAME INDEX

Alexander, J., 42–43, 119n. 22, 134n. 45
Anderson, R. J., 93
Antaki, C., 105
Arendt, H., 13

Bales, R. F., 39
Barnes, B., 38–39, 46, 131n. 19
Becker, H., 130n. 12
Beeghley, L., 118n. 16
Bell, D., 21
Bellah, R., xiii,
Benjamin, W., 12, 114n. 11
Benson, D., 102, 129n. 1
Berger, B., 8
Berger, P. L., xiii, xvi, 5–6, 8, 13, 15–16, 22–25, 29–30, 90, 114n. 8, 116n. 32, 126n. 37
Bergson, H., 126n. 37
Bittner, E., 106
Boden, D., 29
Bourricaud, F., 33–38, 45, 47–49, 118nn. 11, 13
Brittan, A., 122n. 3

Calinescu, M., 114n. 17
Camic, C., 119n. 22
Cicourel, A., 132n. 28

Clayman, S. E., 134n. 45
Collins, R., 55, 73, 78, 128nn. 47, 52, 135n. 49
Coser, R. L., 27
Coulter, J., 91–93
Creelan, P., 54–55, 72–73, 123n. 15, 127n. 41

Dallmayr, F., 4
Durkheim, E., xiii, xvi, 2–4, 55, 99, 118n. 11, 122n. 2, 128n. 47

Eglin, P., 94, 105–06
Eliade, M., 127n. 40
Engels, F., 115n. 18

Fontana, A., 123n. 18
Freud, S., 118n. 12
Friedson, E., 122n. 4
Fromm, E., xvi, 18–19, 27

Garfinkel, H., xvi–xvi, 1, 30, 44, 81–108, 110–112, 119n. 25, 129nn. 4, 5, 130nn. 7, 12, 15, 131nn. 16, 17, 21, 24, 132nn. 28, 34, 133nn. 37, 38, 134nn. 42, 44, 135nn. 46, 47, 48
Geertz, C., 122n. 3

165

SUBJECT INDEX